# Fly High, Land Safely:

## The Definitive Book on Career Transition for Executives

### NESLYN WATSON-DRUÉE

ISBN:9781928155065

PUBLISHED BY:
10-10-10 PUBLISHING
MARKHAM, ON
CANADA

# Contents

# Foreword

Not many of us embrace change with aplomb, let alone grace. That's because change is frightening; it kicks us out of the safe and comfortable into an unknown landscape. After the economic upheaval of the past few years, career change has become the New Normal, and you are likely to change jobs at least 11 times, if statistics are anything to go by. How do you navigate these uncharted waters?

Fly High, Land Safely: The Definitive Guide to Career Transition for Executives by Neslyn Watson-Druée, shows you exactly how to do so, safely, confidently and assuredly. Mixing bite-sized practical advice such as how to network effectively – listening empowers and distinguishing between influencers and followers – with exercises on self-discovery, Neslyn Watson-Druée has produced a book that you want on your desk, and one you would be happy to gift to a friend who is in the midst of or is contemplating change.

Most of you in reacting to change will want to rapidly swap one job for another. Neslyn Watson-Druée however, wisely counsels slowing down to reward yourself with the gift of reflection. Like the rest between musical notes, between the fading echoes of the notes just played and the anticipation of the ones to come, the transition between careers is poignant with potential. Use your time with care that you will make the most life-enhancing decision in moving forward. This is a read to relish and to treasure.

Raymond Aaron
New York Times best-selling Author and Professional Speaker
Double Your Income Doing What You Love

# Chapter 1
# What Leads to Transition

*"If you come to a fork in the road, take it."*
- Yogi Berra

Change is inevitable. It is a given. How you prepare for and cope with change, however, ultimately determines how successful you will be in transitioning from one life situation to another. That is true whether change is occurring in a personal relationship, in a physical location – moving from one home to another, or at work with respect to your career. Change is constant.

However, change and transition are two different things, argues William Bridges in his book, *Transitions*. Change, he says, is what is occurring externally with respect to life circumstances – the new job responsibilities, the new baby, or the new doctor-mandated exercise routine. Transition, however, is the "psychological process" you go through as you process the outward changes. Transitions are "inner reorientation and self-redefinition that you have to go through in order to incorporate any of those changes into your life." I like that definition. To be successful in coping with and adjusting to change, you need to mentally shift how you view the change in order to transition to your new reality.

A transition is a pivotal period of growth and development that is sparked by a change in some aspect of your life. That change is usually a major opportunity, even if it does not appear that way at first. At work especially, if you view change in a positive light, it can lead to fulfilment, personal satisfaction, and new career or personal growth opportunities you could never have imagined.

In your lifetime, you will likely change jobs as many as 15 times, with the average being 11 times by the age of 44, according to the U.S. Bureau of Labor Statistics. Unlike our parents and grandparents, who were likely to work for one employer their entire career and then retire with pension benefits, professionals today do not stay in one place for long. In fact, switching jobs every five to seven years is now typical. Today, career change is the new normal. So whether you are starting to proactively consider where to head next or you are reacting to news that a change to your current employment status is coming whether you like it or not, the key to a successful transition is preparation. Even in reactive mode, there are things you can do to ready yourself for a career or job shift.

**Self-discovery is Key**

Career transition is more a journey of self-discovery than anything else. It is a process of exploring personal strengths and interests, discovering new opportunities, and pursuing a career that is more aligned with each individual's needs and wants. The career goals you may have set for yourself five years ago or even last year, may need to be updated or even overhauled today. As you stop to assess where to go next, you may realise that the path you were on no longer fits you. That is good news.

Realising that another career path will provide you with increased job satisfaction, personal fulfilment, joy, professional challenge, and more, is one of the major benefits of a career transition. Stopping to consider where you are heading, and whether you still like your destination, is wise because it is so much easier to alter course while you are flying than to try and do it once you have landed.

Of course, change and transition are scary. The unknown is scary and, even when you think you know what you want, deciding to take action to pursue it may require a leap of faith. There are generally seven stages that most executives experience as part of a career transition. Some overlap and some do not occur if the transition is forced and not voluntary, but most professionals experience some or all of the following:

## Seven Steps of Career Transition

Change often begins with the seeds of discontent. A certain level of dissatisfaction may begin to emerge that leads to self-reflection, information-gathering and evaluating new challenges and opportunities. Once a better situation is discovered and negotiated, a career transition is completed. But the process starts with a sense that there might be something better out there – something more fulfilling or challenging that you are passionate about.

1. Discontent. Discontent can actually be a two-way street where your employer is concerned. You may be feeling that something is missing, or that things could be better, just as the organisation you are currently working for may be having its own issues of dissatisfaction. Perhaps sales are down, or the company's expansion is not going as planned, or there are lawsuits looming to be dealt with, introducing a sneaking suspicion that change at the top may be needed. Maybe the service values no longer fit with your core beliefs and values.

Either way, the process of questioning what could be starts seeping into your psyche. You may be well-paid, you may have a fabulous office and terrific staff, the work you do may be fulfilling, and yet you may still wonder, "Is this all there is?"

When the discontent is felt by the organisation paying you a salary, you may start to perceive that all is not well. Corporate performance is one gauge, as is employee morale, public news reports and online rumour mills, but board discussions in particular about cutbacks or recent crises can shed light on whether your tenure within an organisation or sector will be short-term or long-term. The signs of an impending parting of the ways usually begin to appear long before the actual event occurs. So watch for them, so that you are not caught off-guard.

The additional challenge with getting fired, sacked, or being made redundant – whatever you prefer to call it – is that you are left feeling that you have no control over your livelihood. You do, of course, have control but, when the decision to leave an employer is not entirely yours, there is a process of grieving that needs to occur before you can move on to subsequent stages in the transition process.

**2. Fear.** What you feel next as you transition is fear – fear of the unknown, fear of what comes next, fear of what may or may not happen and where that will lead you. Change is scary, like I said and, even if you initiate it, moving from the comfortable and familiar to the completely unfamiliar can feel like you are free-falling from a plane. In fact, it is simply turbulence. It is wise to remember that turbulence, while unsettling, is not dangerous as long as you are strapped in well; you are safe.

While you probably do not enjoy being afraid, fear is an important emotion because it can become your propeller to push you forward. When you are afraid, you are also your most creative. If you did not have your current job, what would you do? While your initial instinctive reaction to that question may be fear, you probably moved excitedly on to thoughts of how else you could fill your time. You feel the fear and you move on; you do not let the fear stop you from exploring the future. Do avoid getting stuck.

Once you have control of your fear and put it aside, you can begin to brainstorm all your options, and explore all the alternatives to your current job that are now wide open to you. What a freeing thought. You do not have to land at Heathrow airport or at Gatwick; you can head on to Hamburg or even Helsinki airport, or maybe Paris-Charles de Gaulle. The opportunities are nearly endless. Once you realise that and are ready to truly consider your many options, you have started to move into the next phase.

3. Disconnection. Part of considering the future and where you might be headed – maybe a relocation, a promotion, a year of volunteer work, starting a family, retiring, a sabbatical, the start of a being an entrepreneur – requires that you separate yourself from your former identity. What you were, or what you have left, is your old identity. You are no longer CEO or CFO or director or president or chairman of your organisation. You are now a private citizen with no alliances to contend with – at least for the moment.
In order to move on, you first have to leave behind your former title and role and expectations. You are on your own and, while that may be disconcerting at first, you will quickly get used to it. There are many benefits to being you, an individual, the perfect you.

4. Self-assessment. Having pushed past your former self and your former employer, it is time to take a step back – to take a 35,000 kilometre view of your life and what you want out of it. This is the time to be honest with yourself and with others about:

- your interests and desires
- those life goals you have put off pursuing
- what drives you, what excites you
- what you want to accomplish
- who you want to help
- how you want to help
- where you want to live
- how you want to spend your days?

These are important questions to which you may not have given enough thought.

During the hustle and bustle of daily life you were probably more focused on preparing for meetings or contemplating how to deal with the complex issues within your organisation than with what you are really good at, or what you truly love to do. Fortunately, now that you have decided it is time to move on, to do what you are meant to do, it is time to zero in on what you are passionate about.

Take a moment to reflect on your childhood dreams and desires, what you enjoyed doing at school, or maybe what you excelled at in college or university. What were your thoughts on how you expected to earn a living? What did you love to do? This is the starting point for the direction you should consider taking now. This period of self-reflection and self-assessment is perhaps the most important phase in the entire process of transition. Spend ample time on your reflection; refrain from being rushed.

**5. Exploration.** Having created a list of types of challenges that excite you, or entrepreneurial interest or organisations you would like to be part of, now is the time to look at the viability of those paths in regard to your next job or role. Even if your next position is not a suitable employment position, as you consider all the possibilities available to you, you will want to assess what is possible. That is the focus of this phase – what is out there and what might be right *for you.*

You may discover that the job you had always pictured as being perfect for you, head of a FTSE 100 or a 250 company, for example, may no longer fit your personal needs. In the same way you may find that becoming a year-long volunteer for Greenpeace, which looked so exciting in your 20s, is not quite as appealing or realistic now in your 40s or beyond. That is the value of exploring all of the areas that interest you. You can find out what new situations might be a perfect fit for the person you are now, and you can lay to rest thoughts of employment positions that you have always wondered about, but now see are not as glamorous or high-powered as you had hoped.

By the same token, you may come across opportunities you had not considered or even known were available. Perhaps, in your last role, you were frustrated at your company's unwillingness to invest more in social media, and yet as part of exploring different organisations and openings, you come across a newly-created director of social media at a company that has held your interest, and one in which you would like to work. Or maybe your thoughts of leaving the corporate world to become a coach, develop a business interest or maybe be a full-time writer become more real as you discover writers groups and communal workspaces right in your own backyard.

It is amazing what you may find when you really open your eyes to what is out there. Take the time to explore, to research, to gather information so that you can cull through all that is possible and narrow your focus on what most interests you.

**6. Planning.** When you reach a point where you have narrowed your career options to a handful of opportunities or experiences, it is time to prioritize them. Which one excites you the most? Is it doable? What is your second choice? How do you feel about abandoning your first choice to pursue it? Does it feel right? Which would you regret not going after?

After zeroing in on your next possible path or at least what options you might more fully explore, it is time to start planning. What can you do to more fully investigate or to pursue your top interests? With whom might you network? What events may be of benefit for you to attend? How might you make contact with people who can assist you in transitioning to your next role?

All of those steps or action items are elements of your transition plan. During this phase, you'll begin organising and strategizing how best to pursue your next career opportunity. What are the steps that will get you there most efficiently?

While methodically laying out your path to your next career position is one element of this phase, even more important is your mental and emotional status. Are you feeling optimistic and positive about where you are headed? Are you looking forward to the next stage of your career? Seeing the possibilities and making progress in achieving your goal of a new position is what should be happening here. If you are not feeling good about what comes next, you need to reassess where you are. Maybe the path you are on is not the right one for you.

**7. Transformation.** Although career transition is transformational, that transformation occurs gradually, beginning at your last job and ending when you land a new job that is an even better, more satisfying use of your time and talents. When you reach this phase, you have managed to disconnect from your last position, found a new-and-better role, and are immersing yourself in your career or pursuit. That is the goal for everyone.

Of course, this process of transition does not occur in a matter of hours or days. Disengaging from your former employer and searching for a position that leverages your passion and experience takes time. It also requires support from those around you. Simply switching from one job to another that is quite similar does not qualify as a transition. It takes little thought or soul-searching to accept a promotion or lateral move.

Fortunately, transition is a process that does have a beginning and an end. At the beginning you may be feeling anxious or fearful, but by the end you will be energized, excited, and on a path to a career that is a much better fit for who you are today.

# Chapter 2
# Top Five Reasons for Career Transition

*"If you do what you've always done,*
*you'll get what you've always gotten."*
-Tony Robbins

There are many reasons you may be in transition or considering a career change. You may be unemployed, underemployed, or fully employed but ready for something different. You have been presented with an opportunity. Even executives who are made redundant by their employers or asked to resign are in the same boat; they need to be able to stop for a moment and question what they really want to do next, rather than pursuing the very first job offered to them. If you are in such position it is likely that this will be a pivotal moment in your career, so take your time as you consider your next step.

From my experience as a leadership development consultant and an executive coach, I have identified five main reasons executives decide they are ready for a transition. Some clients find themselves with more than one reason to make a move. They include:

## 1. Wrong job

Perhaps the most common reason senior professionals decide a career transition is needed is being in the wrong job for an extended period of time. The salary may be terrific, the people wonderful, but if you are feeling unfulfilled – that you are not living up to your full potential – or you no longer feel passionate about what you do, it is time to move on. You are not in the right job.

Being in the wrong job can reveal itself in a number of ways. You may decide that your experience or skill-set is not being put to use on a regular basis; for example, being able to apply your financial knowledge from your MBA programme to evaluating the financial sustainability of the company or applying the financial due diligence when considering company mergers, or not being given the opportunity to speak more in public, which you love to do. In these instances, disappointment is felt more than anything else, and maybe a little frustration. The result is that you can imagine a job that you would enjoy more.

Or maybe you feel a sense of boredom, or malaise. You are not happy but you cannot really put your finger on why that is. You may even privately chastise yourself for not appreciating the employment position you currently have. Yet if you are not heading to the office in the morning excited about what the day may bring, something is amiss.

Rather than spending another day, week, or month feeling out of place, stop and take stock of your career, your current position, and the type of role that would be better suited to your strengths.

## 2. Need a bigger challenge

When executives and entrepreneurs get to a point in their careers where they feel they have hit a wall, or a ceiling, the challenge is gone. This frequently occurs when organisations or companies experience a period of rapid growth, followed by a tapering off of activity. The once frantic work environment becomes more tranquil. As service or sales and activity levels off, some executives are left feeling bored.

Having led the organisation or company through the rough seas, the calmer seas can be a let-down.

Or maybe you have climbed to the top of the corporate hierarchy, have spent a few years leading a terrific crew, and now want more. Maybe you have your eye on the chairman's role, or maybe you think it is time to invest your skills in something altogether different. One senior executive I know took a terrific retirement offer, leaving his post at a company at which he had worked for decades, and turned his attention and his resources to starting a local venture fund to assist innovative small businesses get off the ground. Others frequently start new companies, take the helm at larger organisations, or devote their lives to serving the less fortunate. The common theme, however, is the strong desire to feel a sense of purpose as well as having the chance to learn more and build new skills, rather than continuing to apply skills gained long ago.

Even ambitious executives who have quickly climbed the corporate ladder to the top can experience this sense of needing more, once they reach the pinnacle. Some executives experience a sense of mastery and accomplishment after being in a job for a period, while others are already looking to move up another notch on the career ladder, or maybe to get off the ladder and try something completely new. Sometimes a radical departure is the only way for accomplished professionals to find their next calling.

## 3. Being stuck in a rut

For some executives, being made redundant by an employer is a blow to their ego. Although separating from an employer is not a sign of incompetence or weakness, some professionals interpret the action that way; and that is a shame because it is more likely that you, the executive, merely got stuck in a rut. Either the company may have changed around you due to political or economic reasons or you may have stopped developing your own skills and became complacent.

Fortunately, you now have the opportunity to re-educate yourself or to gain skills in an entirely new area that is of interest to you. You may not have enjoyed supervising others in your last job, so now you can strike out on your own as a consultant, coach or freelancer, should you so choose. Or if you were so busy leading and directing the organisation, monitoring the handling of day-to-day matters at your organisation or company that you may never have had a chance to get up-to-speed with technology, now you can.

For other leaders, being stuck in a rut can have more to do with a changing personal life and new responsibilities and a company that is unwilling to be flexible. Such is the case frequently with new parents who find, after their child is born, that being at the office 12 hours a day just does not work any longer. Yet their employer neither has interest in changing their expectations, nor is willing to accommodate flexible working patterns. While the parents may not be in a rut, their employer is, and that affects their career trajectory.

At this point, some – especially women leaders – often elect to step off the career ladder to spend more time with their young children. Not all women do – just look at Marissa Mayer, president of Yahoo! who recently had a child – but those who do find their work-life balance needs have shifted elect to transition out of their current role and into something that better suits their current needs, and that's a good thing. Sticking with a position or company that does not allow you to perform at your best is not good for anyone.

A September 8, 2013 interview in the London *Sunday Times* highlighted Angela Ahrendts, chief executive of Burberry, soon to join Apple Corporation. Angela commented on work-life balance:

> *"It is not possible for female high-flyers to "have it all," and that a balance between work and home is vital. I'm here to run Burberry and I'm here*

*to be a really great wife to my husband. We have three amazing teens, so that's three really big jobs.*

*I don't want to be a great executive without being a great mum and a great wife. I don't want to look back and say I wish I had done things differently. Balance is the really big word for me.*

*ONLY one night out a week, home by Friday night when travelling, and always say no to Oscar invites."*

That is the recipe for a healthy work-life balance from the Burberry chief executive who is one of Britain's best-known and most-admired female bosses.

The *Times* further commented:

Last month Angela Ahrendts spent a Sunday evening with her daughter engrossed in America's Teen Choice awards. I doubt another FTSE 100 boss knows what the event is, let alone watches it, but 53-year-old Ahrendts is a devotee. About 150m teenagers vote online...

## 4. Relocation

In an effort to give senior professionals opportunities to expand their knowledge of the company's operations, many organisations relocate top talent where their skills are needed. This can lead to executives spending 3-5 years in one location, then 3-5 years somewhere else, and so on. Some accept the routine and the process as part of life while others come to a point when they no longer appreciate the constant upheaval. They decide it is time to do things differently.

That can mean refusing future relocation offers, if possible, or negotiating to stay put for a longer period of time – maybe 10 years

– before being asked to uproot again, or quitting to join a company that wants someone to be based locally. There are many possible approaches to dealing with the situation. Ultimately, it will come down to what is best for you going forward.

Others may not mind the relocation process but not be in favour of the city to which they are being asked to move. Leaving London for Exeter, with a population of 111,000, or New York City for Livonia, New York, with 7,809 residents, can be extremely troubling if you are thinking that you might like to eventually settle somewhere. With smaller towns come fewer businesses, especially corporations, and fewer executive positions. Faced with shrinking business opportunities ahead of them, some professionals opt to do something completely different. Instead of relocating, they extricate themselves from the corporate ladder altogether.

## 5. Contribute more

On the other hand, there are executives who have realised that money is not everything and who long for an opportunity to contribute to the greater good or make a difference on a grander scale. If you are in this category of career-changers, you may have become disillusioned with the corporate focus on wealth and profit above all else. These executives are often in search of a way to contribute to the world at large, often in a more hands-on way.

Some executives may decide to volunteer on mission trips overseas to provide support to communities with very little. Others establish charitable foundations or organisations devoted to providing goods or services to those in need right at home. Certain executives may combine their interest in contributing with their corporate skills, and accept a leadership position in the charitable sector or at a non-profit agency. The possibilities are endless but the need for transition is the same – a pure desire to do more for others.

Money at this point is inconsequential. Most executives have all they need and, to that end, what they need now is a way to apply their resources – skills, network, and passion – to enhance the lives of others. That is the type of transition for which they are aiming.

## When is the Right Time?

Now that you have identified why you are in need of change and begun to contemplate what might come next for you career-wise, the next question is, "When is the best time?" That is, when would be an optimal time for you to leave your current position or, if you are already out, when might you start investigating your many options? The short answer is, now.

That is not to suggest that you leave your employment in haste and sell all your belongings for a possible move to Australia. No. Successful transition takes time. It should be approached carefully, thoughtfully, strategically, not reactively or quickly. Jumping from one situation to another without much thought is much like jumping "out of the frying pan and into the fire". It is neither effective nor desirable long-term. You make little progress.

Moving too quickly, you can also run the risk of not fully exploring your interests and alternatives. Rather than move into a new position and discover you are still looking for something else, slow down. Spend far more time gathering information than on rushing to settle on something.

No, not at all; we go through transitions constantly in other areas of our lives. Friends and colleagues transition in and out of our lives over time, children transition into and out of different levels of schooling and, as we progress in learning new skills, like playing an instrument or picking up a new fitness activity, we transition from one level to another and then to another. Transitions are fluid and occur regularly. So it is very possible that one career transition may lead to another.

During this time of reflection, you may realise that you enjoy marketing and public relations so much more than accounting or leading operations, or that you do not enjoy monitoring and supervising as much as you thought you would. So your first career transition may be out of the wrong employment and into a new role at your current company that better meets your needs, or better aligns with your passion, interests, values and abilities.

However, once you have mastered that role, it is possible that in a few years you will be ready for yet another career transition – you may feel a need for a bigger challenge. That may lead you to explore leadership opportunities within your employment sector or within the local community. From there you may realise later that your focus on your company and your career has diminished and you are thinking about giving back to society. There is another opportunity for a career transition that you might never have anticipated.

# Chapter 3
# Life Balance and the Challenge of Transition

*"Balance activity with serenity, wealth with simplicity, persistence with innovation, community with solitude, familiarity with adventure, constancy with change, leading with following."*
- Jonathan Lockwood Huie

Transition is a time of assessment and evaluation, of imagining what could be and then strategizing how to achieve it. Executives for whom work has been their *raison d'etre*, their guiding force, may have a more difficult time picturing life with anything but work in it. When work is everything, and has been for some time, it is harder to picture what else could fit into that life. Leisure activities? Sports? Relationships? Travel? Volunteer work? Social get-togethers? If these kinds of activities and pastimes have been noticeably absent, this transition time is the perfect opportunity to explore reintroducing them for increased satisfaction during transition and after.

Career transition involves more than simply changing your work situation, or how you spend your days. It is about how you spend the rest of your life. So, do you want to continue to spend it as you have been, or is change in order?

The truth is, even if you love your job and have no interest in leaving, it may be possible to find a better balance between your corporate role and your personal life. For some executives, a career transition is either the catalyst for lifestyle changes, or the need for more than work sparks the transition process. Work-life balance leads to increased happiness, fulfilment, and long-term contentment – whether you continue to work or not.

## Signs You Are Approaching Burn-Out

Do you find yourself wishing your day would go faster, or feeling like you are on a treadmill that never seems to take you anywhere? Do you get to the end of the week feeling completely, mentally and emotionally, exhausted, and needing a break? Is getting through the work day getting harder and harder?

If you are more excited to be done with the work day than to get started in the morning, you may be approaching burn-out. That is, your stress level regarding some aspect of your life – often work – is reaching a level that is not healthy. Your work and personal lives are misaligned and out of balance. Unless you make a change, you may soon have health issues or you may reach a point of wanting to quit. Neither of these is a desirable outcome. Improving your work-life balance is important to feeling fulfilled and satisfied about life in general, especially if work has recently become more stressful and less satisfying.

## Achieving Life Balance

Life balance, also known as work-life balance, involves prioritizing your work role and personal life according to what is important to you. For some executives, work may be a very high priority because it provides things like income, power, prestige, and a sense of purpose. Consequently, balance for those individuals may mean working 12-hour days, followed by business dinners, and time spent in the office on the weekends. Especially with younger executives, who may be unattached or not yet parents, or older executives with grown-up children, this time split may work well. However, when responsibilities to others are added to the mix – such as a husband or wife, children, personal causes and volunteering, and/or being a caregiver for an older parent – working 12-hour days may become too stressful. The balance of where time is spent needs to change.

In those scenarios, investing less time on work and more time on outside relationships and activities – shifting where time is spent from the work side of the equation to the personal side – is often needed to achieve balance. Keep in mind that there is no set percentage breakdown that yields balance for everyone; each individual has to set his or her own parameters or guidelines for how much time to give each of their roles. Some executives may be happy with a 60/40 split between time spent working and time spent on personal responsibilities and interests. Others may need 50/50 or 40/60.

Rarely is the division so cut-and-dried, however. We can metamorphose from one role to the next almost fluidly when called upon, such as from CEO to community leader with one phone call, or from chairman to mother on receiving an emergency text from school. This makes assessing exactly what percentage of your day is spent on your various roles a little more challenging, but taking that time to assess where your time is going now is critical. Understanding where you are on the balance continuum now is important to start setting goals for where you want to be.

If 12-hour days at work once worked for you but now eight or 10 hours is plenty, given the other aspects of your life, it is time to rebalance where you are spending your time. Career transitions often involve taking stock of where your time is going and where you would like it to be spent.

## Four Steps to Better Life Balance

Not surprisingly, the process involved in evaluating your existing work-life balance in order to map out a plan for a more harmonious lifestyle mirrors the process required for career transition. Determining what you need, what you want, how you will get there, and how to monitor yourself is the same whether you are taking a closer look at how you spend your time, or assessing whether a career overhaul is in order.

*Step 1: Self-assessment*

As with career planning, the first step in achieving balance is to determine where you are on the life balance continuum. Before you can map out a strategy or plan, you need to know your starting point. So where are you?

- What are your personal strengths and weaknesses?
- What are your interests?
- What kind of training or education have you had that has led you to your current position?
- What types of people do you work best with?
- What types of challenges do you relish? Which do you hate?
- What are the many roles you now hold?
- How do you spend your free time?
- How many hours a week do you invest in leisure and artistic activities?
- How do you feel about the amount of time you currently invest in work?
- What are your major stressors?
- How has that changed in the last year or so?

Once you can get a better sense of who you are right now and how you feel about yourself and your different roles, you are ready to start exploring what life balance could look like. That is, what your many alternatives are.

## Step 2: Discovery

After taking a closer look at where you are right now, and what your life looks like, it is time to explore what kind of lifestyle would be a better fit for your skills, interests, ambitions, and limitations:

- What are your life goals?
- What goals do you want to share with your family?
- What would you change about your current life, if you could?
- When you picture your perfect life, or even just a perfect day, what are you doing? What is your perfect daily life like?
- Does that picture match your life goals?
- What are your different roles?
- Which is the most demanding?
- Which is the most rewarding?
- Are those two roles one and the same? If not, what does that say about your current priorities?
- On what do you wish you could spend more time?
- On what do you wish you could spend less time?

Explore how you could change your current lifestyle to be a better match with the type of person you want to be, the goals you have for yourself, and the life you want to lead. What are some of the changes that would need to occur to get you closer to life balance and happiness (because happiness is a major side effect of having balance in your life)?

## Step 3: Execution

Once you know the areas where you are balanced and imbalanced, do you know where you want to be? Is it time for change? It is time to take steps to effect the change that you have identified? If you have realised that your promotion has meant you are now working 80 hours a week instead of 60 and you are not happy about it, or that the amount of travel you are now having to do for your senior executive role has escalated from 15 percent to 50 percent, and that amount does not fit your life, the first step is to identify what you would like to have happen.

Do you need to become better disciplined yourself about how much you allow work to creep into your down time? Or do you need to set boundaries and expectations for others? And if you are travelling much more than you would like, is there someone on your team to whom you could delegate some of those trips? Is the travel truly essential to your role or your company's performance? How possible is it for you to use technology in some instance to minimise your travel? If the travel is truly essential to your role and your company's performance, then you will need to face the reality and ask yourself if it could ever be possible to achieve the life balance you have outlined; and it may not be.

Now start by writing down the different tasks you need to tackle in order to make changes. Then put them in chronological but escalating order.

Start with having meaningful conversations with the person to whom you report or with colleagues whom you trust. Some discussions may be appropriate for human resources while others may be board-level conversations. Investigate what would need to occur to give you the balance you desire. Do not make ultimatums at this point or threaten any kind of action – merely make inquiries and explore possibilities. What is truly possible? What could be done? Then move that process along as you start to get answers.

Many companies will want to ensure that you are happy and productive; if you are not happy it is likely that your decisions and productivity will have an impact on the bottom line. For that reason companies with emotional resonance will bend over backwards to support you to find a solution, whether that means employing an assistant, setting new work rules and parameters, or creating a new position to assume some of your responsibilities. The options are nearly endless.

Keep pushing until you either get what you need or until you know the changes you need can't be made, and then make a decision about whether you can continue to live your life the way it is currently scheduled; because that's what it comes down to – how you spend the 24 hours in each day.

*Step 4: Monitoring*

If you keep pushing for changes and refuse to stop until your life balance matches your vision of an ideal life, then you will get there. You may have to first go through some turmoil, but you can insist on changes that will be a better fit for your desired lifestyle. Once your life is more balanced and less stressed, the final step is monitoring your success. Check in with yourself regularly to confirm that the balance you have negotiated still fits your current needs. Over time, your definition of life balance is very likely to change as your personal roles change, which means that you'll want to recalibrate where you spend your time, and on what you spend your time. So pay attention to signs of burn-out or stress by asking yourself:

- Is there anything I'd like to do less of?
- What would I like to do more of?
- What is causing me the greatest amount of stress right now?
- Is there anything I can do to easily reduce it?
- Can I delegate some of my responsibilities or employ help to alleviate that stress?
- What do I need today to life a more balanced life that I didn't need six months ago?

Working toward life balance is an ongoing process, which is why it is so important to keep checking back with yourself about how you are feeling about where you are investing your time. You may make improvements, feel completely in control and fulfilled, and then the following month have to deal with a business unit or department that is under investigation by the regulatory or standards authority, or a parent who has become suddenly incapacitated. That life balance you so successfully negotiated, is now gone for the moment, until you cycle through the four-step process again to find out what you need now.

## The Benefits of Leisure and Artistic Interests

Type-A personalities – the people who find great satisfaction and personal reward in work – may recoil at this suggestion, but having interests outside of work is actually good for you and your career. By finding one thing that really excites you and drives you, not only will your stress level decline but you'll become a better performer at your day job. Juggling two important roles makes you better at both, believe it or not. It's like the old adage to give the busiest person you know the most important task, because they are typically the most organised and success-oriented.

There are other benefits to having an outside interest, such as the satisfaction of doing something you love – whether that is playing the cello in a local orchestra, singing in a choir, attending theatre performances or cooking breakfast for the homeless each weekend. Your activity may be simply mixing and mingling with people with whom you might not normally come in contact. It may be a form of networking, but it is much more effective because your motives are pure. More importantly, your efforts to become the best you can be with developing your golf, swimming, walking for pleasure, and exploring new places, or to contribute as much as possible of your own talents to a charitable cause such as improving community literacy, helping the unemployed to find useful employment, or helping the elderly within your community, will help develop a level of confidence and skill that are transferable to your career. It really is a win-win.

## Career Transition is Lifestyle Transition

Creating life balance is an important aspect of career transition. Part of transitioning away from your current role or lifestyle to something new is likely due to your work and personal life not being in sufficient balance. When you find that investment of your time in particular relationships or activities, including work, is not yielding a sufficient return in satisfaction, fulfilment, and pleasure, it is time for a transition. Being out of balance with your career or personal life may suggest that a career transition is needed.

# Chapter 4
## Confidence Helps You Manage Transition

*"Believe you can and you're halfway there."*
- Theodore Roosevelt

Transition of any kind is scary. Moving out of the familiar to the completely unfamiliar is daunting and unsettling. Nonetheless, change, often radical, is what transition is all about. Changing employment, changing careers, changing lifestyles are all transitions and transition takes strength – strength of character and mind-set. Transition requires confidence because the process itself can wear you down and foster doubt and uncertainty. Self-confidence is the antidote. When I speak of self-confidence, I mean your assurance, freedom from doubt, belief in yourself and in your abilities.

If you can picture it, you can attempt and achieve it. Napoleon Hill says, *whatever the mind can conceive and believe, it can achieve.* Self-confidence and self-esteem are not a result of genetics, IQ or luck. They are mental processes and skills which can be learned and developed.

Knowing what you are good at, what you have to offer the world, is the essence of self-confidence. It is a level of comfort with yourself and others that helps you make progress toward goals you have set for yourself. You recognise your goals are realistic and within reach if you strive to achieve them. You know you can do whatever you set out to do.

Martyn Newman in his book – *Emotional Capitalists – The New Leaders* says, 'self-confidence is an emotional component of your personality and the most important factor in determining how you think, feel and behave. Your level of self-confidence largely determines what you make happen in life.'

Your self-confidence is based on your belief in yourself and your abilities, with freedom from doubt as to who you truly are. Self-confidence is about knowing your essence, or the needs, desires, and aspiration of your soul. Self-confidence is your ability to appreciate your perceived positive aspects and possibilities as well as to accept limitations and still feel good about yourself. Self-confidence is the ability to say "I do not know" without feeling inadequate. It is the ability to acknowledge your shortcomings and work towards solutions.

Taking self-confidence to either extreme is, on one hand, boastfulness or arrogance – believing your skills and abilities are better than they actually are– or, on the other hand, low self-esteem, which is, believing you cannot do anything as well as anyone else. It is a position of weakness. Neither arrogance nor low self-esteem is reality, however. To be successful at career transition, you need to find that middle ground. Change is anxiety-producing and nerve-wracking in itself and, to counter it, or cope with it, you need to be confident about your strengths. Your self-assessment should help; there are a range of tools to support you with your self-assessment, and details will be given in the reference section of this book.

Reflecting on where you excel and what you are good at helps you recognise your skills and talents. Not only is this a critical step in the transition process, but it also helps put you in the right frame of mind to make change in your life.

Also, Newman says "self-confidence is made up of three emotional components."

## *Self-Liking*

Self-liking is the "reactor core" of your personality. It is the energy source that determines your levels of self-confidence and enthusiasm. The more you like yourself, the higher the standards you set for yourself. The more you like yourself, the bigger your goals and the longer you will persist in achieving them.

## *Self-Competence*

Self-competence is often called the "inner mirror" – the degree to which you evaluate yourself as competent. It's where you look internally to evaluate your performance in a particular situation. This is so because the power of your self-image is on the outside, so you always consistently act with the picture you have of yourself on the inside.

## *Self- Assurance*

Self-assurance is an attitude that you have towards yourself. When you are self-assured you will remain calm in the face of challenges and you will "look the part" in your chosen role. Newman quotes John Peters, CEO of Technology, Inc.: "You can't lead a cavalry charge if you think you look funny on a horse."

## Tips for Developing Self-Confidence

Fortunately, there are other things you can do to build your self-confidence and maintain it as you evaluate your many career options and zero in on the opportunity that is the best fit.

**Be clear about your strengths and weaknesses.** In the assessment process at the start of your transition, you evaluated what you were good at what you were not so good at. These are your strengths and weaknesses. Hopefully you created a list of 5-10 skills or abilities that you were born with or have developed, as well as 5-10 areas that could use some work, if you wanted to invest the time.

Of course, your list of strengths is much more important than your list of weaknesses. That list is helpful in ensuring you don't pursue employment that expects you to have certain experiences or skills that you lack. Accepting a new position that requires that you apply skills you never bothered to hone because you do not enjoy that kind of work is self-defeating. No one will excel at employment that they hate. Instead, pursue employment and opportunities where you can demonstrate the skills in which you have confidence.

Set a small goal and accomplish it. Nothing builds confidence and poise like tackling a challenge and emerging victorious. Even something as simple as eating five fruits and vegetables a day, which will help to provide long lasting energy, can be a win. Another small win may be your taking action by asking friends or someone who works in the field in which you are applying for a new post to interview you as part of you practising your interviewing skills. **Have conversations** with people who are close to you. Ask them what they see as your personal strengths. Find out why they chose those areas and what it is about you that they think makes you strong in those areas. Self-confidence is largely an awareness skill. Looking at yourself more objectively and honestly is a major step during the transition process.

The key here is to concentrate and focus on your output – what you are responsible for doing – and not the outcome, over which you have little control. Track the number of fruits and vegetables you eat daily so you know when you have hit your target, then celebrate that success. Make a list of all the informational interview requests you have made. Those are achievements, too. Avoid worrying about what may or may not come from those efforts, only about what you are initiating. As you watch the mountain of your success, your self-confidence will grow. What you focus upon will expand in your life.

**Consider your worst-case scenario and develop a Plan B.** Fear gets in the way of going after your dreams. It provides resistance to trying anything new, propelling you into a tizzy that is hard to break free of. So instead of getting worked up about failure, ask yourself, "What is the worst that can happen?" Then talk yourself through the various ways failure could impact your life.

If you are not successful at landing the top-level position at the firm in Paris that you desperately want to work for, what will you do? Is it the end of the world? Hardly. Perhaps your Plan B – your best alternative – is to apply for a position with the company locally so you will be on the short-list for a transfer. Or if Paris is key, perhaps you may consider moving to Paris and then start your employment search. Your worst case probably may not look so terrible once you break it down.

Or if your goal is to start your own business but you are afraid of failing, describe what that would mean. Would it mean investing your savings in the venture and losing it? Would it mean embarrassment? What is the worst that could happen? Actually, if the worst happens and the business does not survive, most entrepreneurs go on to establish second and third and fourth ventures. If you are an entrepreneur, it is likely you will fail with some of your undertakings, and that's okay. But if your savings are depleted, what is your Plan B? You likely have a number of options, including going back to a corporate position or even getting a job with a company similar to the one you wanted to start. Failing in business is certainly not the worst situation, and this exercise is designed to make you aware of that fact.

If you can imagine the worst-case and recognise it's not so bad, your confidence in yourself and your idea will be bolstered.

**Mentally review past successes.** Whenever you begin to question whether your goals are realistic or if your transition will take you where you want to go, think back on challenges you have faced in the past where you were successful. Were you fast-tracked for your company's management training programme only six months after working there? Did you win top salesperson of the year two years in a row? Was your volunteer work on a non-profit's grant application pivotal to their winning the grant? What are some of the accomplishments you are most proud of?

Especially recall situations where success was far from given – when it looked extremely unlikely – and yet your skills saved the day. Remembering situations that were uphill battles and where you were still victorious, or where the challenge looked insurmountable at first, is a good way to remind you of your capabilities and talents. Past successes are confidence builders.

**Join a transition group or support group.** Being able to admit your fears and concerns to others who are going through the same transition process can be both comforting and reassuring. Discussions and meetings with similarly-situated professionals and executives can offer positive reinforcement when you may need it. You may also find such a group useful for brainstorming new ideas, new approaches to making contacts, or locating helpful resources.

Your employer may offer such a group, an executive recruiting firm may have something, or a career counselling practice may be able to connect you to a group of fellow top-level executives.

## Strategies for Fending Off Doubt

Just as you work to boost your self-confidence in preparation for the next phase of your career and life, it is also helpful if you stop doing other things. The opposite of self-confidence is self-doubt and, where doubt exists, you will have a harder time achieving success. Bear the following five suggestions in mind:

**Consider change as growth.** Staying in the same employment position at the same company for your entire career does not create a happy and fulfilled employee. Change is good. It challenges you to learn, to adapt, to stretch mental muscles you may not have used in some time. Is it okay to be afraid? Absolutely, but cease from letting fear overtake your career. It is best not to fear change. Steering clear of change will not enhance your self-confidence; it will only foster self-criticism and self-doubt.

**Results are cumulative.** Transition is a process that takes time, much like other important aspects of life. Settling in to a new city or a new country, learning a foreign language, establishing new peer relationships at work, or improving your self-confidence – these do not happen overnight. They take effort, focus, and time. When you expect or demand immediate results of yourself, you damage your self-confidence. Instead, be patient. Give yourself time to achieve results.

**Focus on what you can control.** If something is beyond your control, such as a recruitment decision or request for a recommendation, stop worrying about it. Focus on why you may be employed rather than reviewing all the reasons you may not secure the position or why your former boss may not endorse you. There is no point. Not only do you have no control over what happens, but fretting over what may or may not happen only serves to damage your self-confidence. Focus instead on what you can control, such as your actions, your efforts, and your responses to others.

**It is challenging to please others all the time.** The first reason is that it is impossible to please everyone all the time. Instead, stay focused on your own goals and values and pay attention to your own needs while being emotionally aware of how your thoughts and feelings are impacting others. This does not mean changing your thoughts, but for you to be adept in leveraging how you present your thoughts and feelings to others so that you are heard. Staying true to what you know to be the right decision for you builds your self-confidence and allows you to maintain control of your image and your reaction to those around you. If you allow others to dictate how you should act, the decisions you should make, or what is important to you, your own self-confidence is entirely out of your hands. In reality, what others say should not matter to you at all. It really has nothing to do with you.

**Celebrate the successes of others.** Just as it is important not to pay attention to what others may or may not be saying about you, it is essential to see the success of others as if those successes were your own. The success that others attain has everything to do with them, their skills and efforts, and next to nothing to do with you. So celebrate their success!

Congratulate colleagues when they are successful. Not only is it kind and polite, but it demonstrates that you are confident enough in your own abilities to pat someone else on the back. Insecure and needy people, who are threatened by someone else's success, tend to be envious of the success of others without being sufficiently aware that the success of others has nothing to do with them. Having friends and colleagues who are successful does not mean you are any less successful – only that you hang out with like-minded professionals. That is a good thing.

## The Cycle of Confidence

Just as success breeds success, confidence breeds confidence, and promotions. The more confident you come across, the more confidence others have in you, which has been associated with greater upward mobility. People are much more comfortable backing someone who presents ideas with confidence and assuredness than someone who appears nervous and unsure.

# Chapter 5
# Managing Expectations

*"If you paint in your mind a picture of bright and happy expectations,*
*you put yourself into a condition conducive to your goal."*
- Norman Vincent Peale

We all have expectations of how we want our lives to be. They include career expectations, relationship expectations, lifestyle expectations, income expectations, and more. Based on what we know about ourselves, we expect success. While having goals in mind is always helpful in achieving them, those goals also need to be reasonable. Expectations need to be based in reality in order to be helpful; otherwise, they can be damaging. This is true of expectations you set for yourself as well as expectations others have of you, or expectations you have of them.

Unfortunately, expectations are frequently subconscious. Expectations are your vision of a future state or action, usually unstated but which is critical to your success. In your mind, satisfaction is how closely you have come to your expectation. When my clients express disappointment about an outcome, I probe three areas. What expectations did you set in the beginning? Based on the presented reality, how closely did you monitor your expectations? What were your thoughts and what did you do to influence your expectations?

You may have given a brilliant presentation but, if you have not managed the expectations of others as well as monitored how your presentation is being received and show sufficient connection to your audience's expectation, it is likely that you will experience disappointment.

You may also have subconscious expectations of others, such as expecting to be asked by a group of friends to go on holiday together again this year, or expecting that the employee you are mentoring would ask more advice from you. When people do not live up to your expectations, it may have an impact on your self-confidence, or simply leave you feeling let down.

The only way to avert such situations is to try and bring any and all expectations to the forefront, to the conscious mind, so that you are clear about them with yourself and with others. This is what managing expectations is all about – consciously setting them and communicating them so that no one is disappointed.

Managing expectations is important during a career transition so that you end up with a new position that is well suited for you. Setting your sights on a position that is completely wrong for you is not productive, nor will it lead to happiness and fulfilment – the goals of a successful transition.

## Setting and Managing Your Own Expectations

It is only natural to want the best for yourself. We all feel that way, which is why setting goals is so important. You want to set expectations for your own performance that provide a path to success. When you do not live up to your own expectations, you experience guilt, frustration, anger, and sadness – emotions no one wants to feel. Conversely, when you exceed expectations, you feel confident, satisfied, and happy.

Since self-confidence has been shown to increase or enhance career success, setting reasonable goals that you can realistically meet or exceed is likely to yield positive career results. That is the essence of managing expectations – reducing or eliminating the difference between what we expect and what we get.

But what are reasonable expectations? During career transition, when uncertainty is the norm, it is important to be clear about your goals. If you are currently unemployed and hunting for that next position, you may set goals regarding contacts made, emails sent, job listings responded to. When you quantify your goals, you create a way to evaluate your performance. So if your goal was to make 20 new contacts this week and you made only 15, you did not meet your expectations. But instead of becoming angry and upset, step back for a moment and review why that occurred. Take the opportunity to learn from this situation.

Was it unrealistic to expect yourself to have time to reach out to 20 people, given other interviews and appointments you already had scheduled? Did another opportunity come up that you needed to invest time in researching, taking away time from outreach? Or are you questioning whether this is the right approach to your next career move? All of these are important questions that you'll want to mull before proceeding.

While you want to set goals and expectations that propel you to greater success, it is also important to be realistic. Setting expectations that are beyond the realm of possibility is futile, frustrating, and a waste of time. It would be like planning to fly to the moon in your private jet – it's not going to happen no matter how much extra fuel you add to the tank.

So rather than randomly stating an intention to have a new position in four weeks, research the average amount of time it takes someone

41

at your level to move to the next desired position. It may be twelve weeks, or it may be six months. The point is to set expectations that are based in reality rather than on what would be most convenient for you. Give yourself extra time to scan the environment, do a reality check, assess your skills and your situation, and develop a plan for securing your next position, whatever it is. Allow yourself this time to truly consider all of the things you are truly passionate about. Only when you have reached a point of feeling that you have explored all of the relevant options should you start tapering on specific opportunities.

Rushing yourself through any transition, whether it is mental, physical, or emotional, eventually prolongs the transition or causes more hurt. Accept that assessing, discovering, executing, and monitoring will take much longer, on average, than what you initially expect. So, to be safe, double your initial estimates. That way, if it takes you less time, you will exceed your own expectations and everyone else's. But if you state that you will spend two months on a career assessment and you end up taking five, you and everyone around you may start to feel anxious that it's taking so long. Instead, allow for lots of extra time. It will reduce everyone's stress levels by lowering their expectations of you and the time required for this important process.

Most importantly, avoid setting yourself up to fail. That will happen when you fall short of your initial expectations. During this time of self-reflection and exploration, try and steer clear of setting goals that are too demanding or are out of your control, such as waiting for responses from others. Finding the right position is infinitely more important than taking any position that is presented to you in the short term, and that takes time.

## Setting Family Expectations

Members of your immediate family may be unnerved when they hear the news that you are in career transition and that you are evaluating your next career move. They are used to life the way it has been, and they have become accustomed to what is familiar. There is a rhythm and daily routine, and they have inured themselves to what appears comfortable, and hence they may resist change.

It is as if you have told your family that you are all taking a trip to South Africa. Everyone is excited. You pack, you get on the plane, you head out over the Middle East and then, as you reach African airspace, you announce that you have decided you would rather go cruising in the Caribbean. "Huh?!" Your family reacts.

You will land, but it may not be safely. Your abrupt change in flight plan may cause a mid-air ruckus, just as news of the impact of your career transition on your family may cause a ruckus as well.

Although your family might have loved the idea of cruising if you had presented it originally, they expected to land in warm Barbados. You set the expectation of a certain kind of trip and then you changed course, disrupting their plans and enjoyment. That is a little of what your career transition is for them.

*You* might be perfectly happy to go to Los Angeles, or Canada, or Madrid, or Edinburgh, but your family may have other preferences, so you need to sort those out as part of your transition. Just as you evaluated your personal strengths and weaknesses, likes and dislikes, so too is the preparation of your family so that you get to understand their lifestyle preferences before you need to make a final decision about where you position yourself.

This might include where you live, the kind of home you live in, the amount of time you have to spend with your family, and the amount of disposable income you all have to enjoy. Any career change will have an impact on every aspect of your life, including your family's; therefore, you need to set the expectations for them. If you decide to switch industries, moving from a fast-paced, 24/7 work day to one where executives are encouraged to have a home life – or vice versa – your family needs to understand how that shift will affect them. Or if you are pondering leaving corporate life to teach at a university, where you would have summers relatively free of work but earn a smaller salary, your family needs to be prepared for that eventuality, too.

They may be happy with whatever choice you make, but I can almost guarantee that they will not be happy if you fail to communicate possible changes. Set the expectation up front regarding what changes may occur and you will avoid imposing feelings of frustration, anger, and disappointment on those around you when things do not go the way they expected them to.

Setting expectations is important now, as you transition from your old position to something new – whatever that is. If you have left your employment, explain what life will be like for a short while as you explore your options. If you are still working but intend to move to something else, you may or may not want to share that with children – it might be best to wait until you know what you will be doing next. As soon as you have discovered where you are meant to go next, then let your family know that too, as well as what it will take to help you get started on that journey.

Most families are very supportive of your choices but they also appreciate being part of the decision-making process, or at least being given a heads up that they soon will be transitioning too. It is best not to land a surprise on your family.

## Managing the Expectations of Peers and Colleagues

Some say that friends are the family you choose, so it is no surprise that they may have their own expectations for you. Close friends want you to be happy. True friends support the choices you have made and are making now to get there. Colleagues and peers at work are not as invested in your happiness and success as your closest friends but they may be affected by your transition nonetheless. Those who report directly to you especially will be impacted by any steps you take to assess your career trajectory and your decisions regarding where you prefer to land.

While your peers may offer advice and counsel regarding your next step, be aware that they are biased – they have a stake in your success. Keep this fact that they may be subjective, not objective, in the back of your mind as you ask for opinions and observations from them. Once you leave your current position, there will be jockeying amongst those remaining for who will fill your role. Some may want you to step aside sooner rather than later in the hopes of being given your current position. Your allies may not want you to leave at all, for fear that their future prospects will be dampened by your absence. Others around you may expect you to take a promotion elsewhere, or to jump ship to go running your own business or even to undertake a course of study. These are expectations that others may have for you – some good, some unrealistic and some indifferent. Underlying those expectations are personal desires and ambitions, rather than concern for your well-being.

This is a rather long way of sharing with you that, with the exception of your immediate family and perhaps your best friends, no one else's expectations should matter. The whole reason you have initiated a career transition is to make change – change that may not be comfortable for everyone. Yet it is important for you to listen to your heart. Be clear about what will make you happy and stick to that flight plan.

45

# Chapter 6
# Knowing Yourself

*"People have several times more potential for growth
when they invest their energy in developing their strengths
instead of correcting their deficiencies."*
- Tom Rath in *StrengthsFinder 2.0*

Feeling successful, satisfied, and energised professionally requires knowledge – knowledge of yourself. Without a familiarity with, or level of awareness of, your preferences, dislikes, strengths, and weaknesses, it is nearly impossible to choose a career path that will make you happy long term. How can you make the most of your skills and abilities if you are not even sure what they are?! Finding a profession or purpose that is personally fulfilling is that much more challenging as well.

Unfortunately, most of us focus far too much attention on our weaknesses, rather than our strengths. We take our strengths, our skills, for granted, believing that what we do best is nothing special – everyone has the same talents, we are sure – when, in fact, very few people have the same combination of capabilities. The key to your personal and professional success is recognising your strengths, highlighting them for professional gain, and timing major career moves to make the most of opportunities that arise. That combination of self-knowledge, strengths awareness, and timing that can lead to tremendous success.

## Redirecting your focus

Since primary school, we have been trained to identify and improve our weaknesses. During school, our parents and teachers were constantly on alert to spot any difficulties in learning new material. Any apparent lack of understanding of words, or mathematics, or science led teachers to suggest or provide additional materials to help remedy the situation. Students were all expected to learn at the same relative pace, apparently, and anyone who lagged slightly stood out.

Tom Rath provided a powerful illustration of a real life story from Gallup's economic development work in Puebla, Mexico, of what can happen when people focus on their natural talents. Hector had been known as a great shoemaker. International customers claimed that Hector made the best shoes in the world. Yet for years, Hector had been frustrated with his shoe-making business. Although he knew he was capable of making hundreds of shoes per week, on average he was making just 30 pairs. A friend of Hector asked why this was so. Hector explained that, while he was great at producing shoes, he was a poor salesman and even worse when it came to collecting payments. Yet Hector spent most of his time working in these areas of weakness.

Hector's friend introduced him to a natural salesman and marketer who agreed to work with Hector. One year later, leveraging each other's strengths, Hector and Sergio, the salesman and marketer, were producing, selling, and collecting payment for more than 100 pairs of shoes per week. The maxim of the story is: *You **cannot** be anything you want to be – but you can be a lot more of who you already are.*

The following comments are representative of focusing on strengths: *I sincerely believe in '**Play to your strengths.**' One could become mediocre when he/she focuses on weakness, but focusing on strengths can only take people to excellence.* Sivakumar Palaniappan

*I have tried for years and years to work on my weaknesses and improve what I was not good at. I have to say I did grow and improve, but my growth was at a very slow rate and with gains that did not meet my expectations. I was still 'not good' at what I used to be bad at. Basically, focusing on improving my weaknesses took a lot of my energy, time and attention away from excelling in my career. I truly believe that it is one's strength that moves you ahead in your career.* Oneya Salem

*I think it would help a lot of people to focus on/play to their strengths. They would find better direction for their lives.* Susie Smith

The fact is, it is much more difficult to shore up or eliminate your weakness than it is to fortify your strength. Investing time and energy in trying to build up non-existent skills is wasteful when it is far easier to amplify an existing forté. Your career does not depend on how well you address your weaknesses – it depends on how well you make use of your strengths.

*I find us to be a nation that focuses on the negative. Imagine what our outcome would be, the bottom line result, the revenue generated, should we finally begin to focus on our strengths and what we do right and begin to believe in possibilities.* Pamela Horton

While most professionals find it challenging to point out their own strengths, since you have already assessed your own strengths and weaknesses you have an advantage.

**Taking stock of your UBS**

Planning for your future takes UBS – Understanding your circumstances, Believing in your strengths, and Sensing your intuition. These three elements together can make the difference between a satisfactory career and a deeply fulfilling, exciting work-life doing whatever it is that makes you most happy. Wouldn't you prefer to spend your days "working" doing something you absolutely love? To do that, you need to take a close look at your UBS.

*Understanding your circumstances*

Knowing yourself requires that you recognise what you want as well as why you want it. Of course, why you want it is an infinitely more important question because the answer says so much more about you as a person. For example, do you aspire to earn £1,000,000 per year because you:

- Want a comfortable lifestyle for your family?
- Dream of establishing a charitable foundation to make a difference in the world?
- See it as a stepping stone to starting your own business?
- Aspire to becoming an angel investor and investing in other small businesses?

These are all potential answers to your "why".

Or perhaps you are looking for a new position in finance (that is the "what" of your circumstances)

- because you were recently made redundant.
- because you elected to retire early, or
- because you no longer felt challenged in your old role in manufacturing (these are the possible "whys" of your circumstances).

Be honest with yourself here. If need be, be brutally honest. Only through honesty can you find what you were truly meant to do. To pretend that job titles no longer matter (when they really do), or that the type of organisation you work for is immaterial (when you really, really want to be in the world of fashion and design), or that you have no preference regarding the type of client you serve (when you are truly passionate about helping teenagers), will waste everyone's time and you will end up in a role that you are not ideally suited for.

Understand your circumstances and be clear about how you picture your ideal life – personally and professionally. This kind of clarity will only help open doors and lead you to what you are meant to do next.

## Belief in your strengths

Discovering what your strengths are, either by completing an assessment that indicates what they are or by asking others for feedback, is important. Believing and internalising that knowledge is critical. You may hear from those around you that you are a top-notch retailer or that you have the ability to bring products to market like no other but, until you accept and believe what you are hearing, you are not ready to make full use of those strengths.

Perhaps you simply do not believe that you possess a particular skill, or you feel that your mastery of it is far from exceptional. Whatever it is that you are telling yourself, stop it! If someone remarks that you are adept at calming potentially explosive situations, stop and think about what you have just heard. Few people offer specific positive feedback unless it is well-earned. Is it possible that you are able to facilitate peace in the boardroom better than most? If you have heard it more than a couple of times, consider that your colleagues or friends may be right. Instead of resisting the observation or compliment, try accepting it and believing it. It may lead you to a new career path.

## Sensing your intuition

We all have intuition – that internal "gut feel" about situations or people that seems to emerge from our subconscious. Intuition is subconscious knowledge, or knowing without being aware that you know, that emerges as a feeling rather than a conscious thought. Some people either ignore their intuition or have difficulty recognising it, while others are attuned to their intuition and let it guide their decisions. Surprisingly, intuition has been linked to career success.

To harness your intuition, you first need to identify what it is that you want in the way of a career – to be clear about the position or role you want. You have already done this through your self-assessment, so you should be able to imagine what that new position looks like. Having visualised the next step on your journey, let your intuition present you with opportunities to acquire your desired position. Be aware of sensations that indicate a person or opportunity or action will lead you down the right path or the wrong path. Your intuition will steer you if you pay attention.

**Doing what you love to do**

Knowing your strengths and being willing to emphasize them is central to finding career success in a field or position you love. Finding your strengths is invaluable in a number of ways in leading you to the right opportunities and making you stand out when you apply for them.

Knowing what you are good at, and what kind of position you want for yourself, is extremely useful in focusing your career transition. Understanding that one of your strengths is creativity and finding creative solutions to manufacturing problems, for example, will lead you in a direction towards opportunities that will make the most of that strength, such as in consulting or operations. This knowledge helps refine your search, limiting the scope and helping to eliminate positions for which you are not the best choice.

That understanding of your strengths also makes it possible for you to highlight and emphasize them when applying for a new position. Being able to point to instances when you leveraged your knowledge of statistics to help your employer will undoubtedly make you stand out when compared to other candidates applying for the same position in marketing analysis. Or telling stories of your ability to clinch major contracts for the business development team will surely make you a more desirable candidate for a management role in business development than someone who has not had your successes. Make sure your strengths are obvious to your potential employer and you will significantly increase your odds of being appointed to the position for which you are applying.

Being clear about your strengths is also helpful during employment interviews, giving you a level of confidence and self-assuredness that will make you even more attractive. Look for opportunities to discuss your strengths during such interviews, or to answer questions in such a way that your strengths are clear. When compared to others who are applying for the same position, you will come across as much more accomplished and experienced simply by knowing and communicating your strengths to others.

Knowing your strengths prepares you to take advantage of any opportunity that comes along that will help you make better use of your strengths, but timing always plays a role as well.

**Timing your career transition**

Jumping at the first offer that comes along and appears to be a better fit for your goals and interests may not be the best move long term. Timing makes all the difference between a success and an unmitigated disaster, even when you are fully aware of your strengths.

Relating to insight from John Maxwell in his book – *The 21 Irrefutable Laws Of Leadership,* when you make a career move – any kind of move – there are four possible outcomes:

- The wrong move at the wrong time is typically disastrous in the short and long term.
- The right move at the wrong time can cause resistance from those around you, including a significant other.
- The wrong move at the right time is always a mistake, mainly because there is never a right time to make a bad move.
- The right move at the right time can yield continued success.

So how do you know which of these scenarios you are facing? You need to evaluate both factors – the position itself and the timing of your move. In all cases, making the right move is most important. Finding a position that plays to your strengths within an organisation that can make the most of your talents and clearly recognises all that you bring to the table is your ultimate goal, whether the organisation happens to be a multi-national corporation, a new start-up, or a charity with a mission that speaks to your heart. Where you land is secondary to finding a role where you can contribute and grow as a person. However, finding that position that maximizes your strengths may take time.

As you observe that you are becoming impatient and anxious, try and remind yourself that making a move simply for the sake of change often leads to failure. Taking a position that you know intuitively is not the right one – not the one you were meant to have or could have – will only leave you feeling disappointed and resentful when the right one comes along and you are not prepared to take it. Accepting the wrong position and agreeing to a year-long contract means that you are locked in no matter what else comes along; think long and hard before closing off all other employment offers if you know the current opportunity is not all that you had imagined. Patience and timing are closely related.

Likewise, accepting a position at a time when leaving your former employer will cause chaos and disruption and potentially damage your professional reputation is a mistake that could have longer-lasting repercussions than you could imagine. Or accepting the perfect position, which, unfortunately, is located hundreds of miles away, could put your marriage or serious relationship at risk. Make sure you are certain the position is worth wreaking all that havoc for.

Of course, if you can get the timing right, you will find the right position and be ready and available to accept it. That means finding a role that plays to your strengths, in an organisation that appeals to you, at a time when you are ready and available to take it. That is the epitome of success.

# Chapter 7
# Defining Success

*"Success is not the key to happiness. Happiness is the key to success. If you love what you are doing, you will be successful."*
- Albert Schweitzer

Transition is a time for reflection, for introspection, and for evaluating what success would look like to you now. In order to effectively reorient your life to provide you the happiness and satisfaction you want and deserve, it is important to decide exactly what it is that you want your life to look like. Otherwise, you run the risk of pursuing new positions or career situations that will only make you miserable. That is not a successful career transition. A successful career transition ultimately leaves you in a vocation that is perfectly aligned with your goals and definition of success. However, to do that you need to be clear about what it would mean for you to be successful, including what that means today.

That is an important question because our definition of success changes over time. Your definition of success today is likely to look quite different from that same definition five or ten years ago. It changes due to career experience and achievement, as well as due to changes in personal priorities and family life. What might have seemed the epitome of success in your 20s, such as being promoted to partner or buying a Mercedes-Benz, may seem much less important or significant once accomplished. Your goals and vision of success in your 30s, 40s, 50s, and 60s may be very different from your aspirations right out of university. Or perhaps your goals remain the same. Either way, it is smart to stop and decide what it is you are working toward now, before you start out on a new path.

Every individual has his or her own definition of success. Some equate success with financial wealth and all that money can buy, such as ornate houses, expensive cars, designer clothing, international vacations, and the like. Others define success based on their achievement of personal goals, such as being named a corporate director by a certain age, being hired by a prestigious firm, reaching a particular salary grade, or being appointed to a government position. Or having peace of mind, successful relationships and family may be the driver. A number of my clients tell me that success for them is the degree to which they are happy with a partner, getting married, and having children. All of the aforementioned could be your definition of success – there is no right or wrong answer. However, to transition to a new and better career, it is important to be crystal clear about where you are headed and why.

## Identifying your "why"

So, start by defining what success means to you. Then ask yourself why you want that particular picture of success. If success is earning one hundred thousand pounds per year or more, ask yourself, why that amount is significant? What would that amount of income mean for you and your family? Why, exactly, do you want to earn that amount of money?

The answer might be that being successful by earning a lot of money will allow you more freedom or allow you to give your children particular education, or to set up a scholarship in honour of your parents, or to retire in a few years and move to a warmer climate. This answer – your "why" – is your true definition of success. In this example, the money you earn is the tool that allows you to be successful, but in and of itself the money is not what is important.

Likewise, if you believe being successful comes only from achieving a certain title at work, think about why that title is so important. What is so different about being a company director, chief operating officer, CEO, chairman or president? Besides money, what is it about the title that means so much to you? Is it the respect or admiration you anticipate colleagues feeling toward you? Is it the new employment opportunities that may come your way, or the invitations to serve on other boards of directors? Why is that title so important? Once you dig down to the real purpose of obtaining that title, or whatever your definition of success is, you are better prepared for career transition.

## A new definition of success

The real message here, which you may have already realised, is that achievement and success are two different things. Achievement is an end result and success is a process. Yes, a promotion is an accomplishment, for example, and something to be proud of to be sure, but are you successful if you earn a promotion? Maybe and maybe not; the answer depends on your potential and capabilities. Earning a promotion in a position you are overqualified for is almost meaningless, but a promotion that is the result of your best efforts and hard work certainly is an indication of success.

Does being made redundant mean you are not successful? Not at all; in some respects redundancy may be a blessing because it may leverage you to take the step to engage with your passion and ideal interests. You may be out of employment because you were not right for the position. There is no shame in that; so now you have the chance to look for and find a spot that give you the perfect opportunity to apply your knowledge, skills and abilities. When that happens, you will most definitely be successful.

That is because being successful is about how you act or react in a given situation. Faced with hardship, do you crumble and give up or do you look inward to determine how to get out of the tight spot you are in? Success is doing the best you can, even when dealing with unexpected or bad news. Successful people look for ways to overcome challenges, whether they are financial or employment-related or personal, and persevere until they are happy with where they end up. Those are the success stories. But while you are hunting for that better employment or better match with your personal goals you are also a success, because you are doing your best to improve your life. You are being proactive, not waiting for someone else to take the reins and turn things around for you.

The fact that you have not quit and that you continue to pursue your personal goals, makes you successful. Success is the progress you have made from being where you were to where you are now. It is the difference between knowing you were ready for a change to meeting with a career coach to explore where you go next. It is the difference between being upset about being made redundant to sending out resumés and cover letters to inquire about current employment openings. It is the difference between staying in an employment position that bores you and registering for personal development courses, or courses to earn a Master's degree. Success is the action you take to transition from what is not working for you in your career to what you were meant to do.

## Taking charge of your future

If success is based on action, on moving forward, then planning what you will do next is certainly successful behaviour. Charting your career course will lead you to what you were meant to do, whether that is to change employment, change employers, change industries, or change continents. Anything is possible once you determine what success means for you. In a group coaching session, I remember Andy Harrington, CEO and founder of The Public Speaking University, saying: *'Most people count the cost of moving forward but never count the cost of standing still. In moving forward you pay once; in standing still you pay forever with feelings of regret, wondering what might have been or blaming others for your inaction to do the right thing for you.'*

There is, however, another side of the coin to consider. How will your move forward affect those around you? As an executive, it is likely that you have a staff that reports to you – how will their jobs be impacted by your transition? What can you do to ensure that they can continue to do their jobs to the best of their ability after you leave? Even if you do not have a staff, anticipating what you can do to help minimize the possible disappointment that your leaving will cause at your current employer will ensure you leave on good terms. Your moving on may cause disruption, but it need not be a negative event. To avoid difficulties, you will want to start thinking about succession planning (notice how "success" is a critical piece of that phrase).

You have no doubt heard the phrase "succession planning", most likely as it relates to planning for the next generation of leaders at your employer. Businesses often develop long-term plans for their leadership ranks, to ensure any changes will have relatively little impact on the company's operations. Succession planning, however, should not be limited only to executive directors and CEOs. Planning for who will succeed you, that is, replace you or take over your responsibilities, makes sense for organisations and individuals at all levels. The more thought invested early on, the fewer the difficulties when employee changes do occur.

Charlie Wagstaff, Criticaleye co-founder says, *if you are a CEO, it is important to view succession as a critical part of your role. Part of your competence as a successful CEO is your ability to create and develop a top team that is allied to the future capability requirements of your organisation.* You may well ask – to what extent should you as the CEO nurture the process of succession in your organisation?

In addition, Wagstaff says, *'while there's no reason why your company's success should not continue under a changed leader, a smooth transition will frequently depend upon the quality of your top management team. To that extent, you as the CEO have a dynamic role to play, not only as the organisation's current leader but also as steward of its future direction.'*

In your business, your key role as the CEO involves the consideration of the long-term strategic objectives for the business and, within this, how to develop a team that can maintain the growth of the business when you move on.

Kai Peters, chief executive of Ashridge, the business school located in Berkhamsted, near London, says that: *"The CEO sees within his/her organisation that there are many talented individuals, each with a role to play and some who have the ability to fulfil many important leading roles. The CEO, as steward of the organisation, is clearly interested in having the best people possible to achieve the strategic goals that have been identified."*

**Planning for your successor**

As you begin to chart your next career, or to decide what to do after you stop working, it may help both your employer and you if you do some succession planning. Perhaps surprisingly, some executives and entrepreneurs often have difficulty separating themselves from the organisations they have led, thinking that no one else can run them as well as they can. Even after expressing excitement for the next phase of their lives, some managers and leaders still find it painful to leave behind the work life they have known for years. It is important to know that taking the time to identify and mentor appropriate replacements allows leaders to walk away confidently, knowing they have groomed a strong person to fill their shoes. The major benefit of succession planning relates to the ability to hand-pick and advise suitable replacement before stepping aside. It leaves the organisation stronger and provides a means for executives to shift their focus away from their former role.

Because it provides a "hand-off" from one leader to another, succession planning is both good for a company and good for the transitioning executive. Having chosen a talented successor, executives can start investing their time and attention on what comes next, rather than on worrying about what they are leaving behind; leaders who have spent most of their careers in one organisation may find this especially difficult. Additionally, their employer can continue to function with little downtime or disruption due to a change in management.

While an executive may be seeking a transition to something else, their employer may have no inkling that a change will soon be necessary. Succession planning can reduce concern about who would take over should someone leave, reassuring investors, employees, and customers when such a time does come.

To allow time for you, the employee, to create your own definition of success and to evaluate what your next career stage might be, consider starting the succession planning process months or years before you anticipate stepping aside. Your company may have its own succession planning process for executive-level positions, but you too can do your own behind-the-scenes planning. Before your plan to leave is announced or made public, begin to consider how to help your organisation find a strong successor.

The most important steps in the process include:

- **Developing a five-year business plan for the organisation.** Make sure there is a corporate-level or business unit-level plan to guide the company, no matter who is in charge. This should include revenue targets, operational goals, and growth plans that lay out a strategy for the business to follow.
- **Creating key role descriptions**. Before you go hunting for individuals to fill important roles, describe the experiences,

skill-sets, and personalities you believe will be most successful for the role. What are the key responsibilities of each position? What kind of individual is likely to succeed in such a role?

- **Identifying high potential candidates for future leadership roles.** Once you know what kind of leaders you are looking for, you can now try and match existing employees who have the potential to grow into executive roles, as well as identifying areas where outside candidates should be considered. Many companies create organisational charts with potential successors identified by name.
- **Forging mentor relationships.** Employees likely to be tapped for managerial roles down the line could benefit greatly from regular mentoring or coaching from senior managers. Explore ways you can mentor junior leaders within your organisation, in order to better prepare them for future leadership responsibilities.
- **Establishing a timeline for your departure.** Once you have made the decision to leave, work with your management team to detail a schedule outlining key milestones associated with your exit. The more time allotted for this process, the better – six months to a year is not too long.

Not only is succession planning important and useful for the business, but it allows executives the opportunity to continue to shape the company even after you leave. By helping to set the stage for future growth and selecting managers who have the qualifications and skills you believe necessary to be successful in a particular role, you can leave the company in better shape than when you arrived. There should be a feeling of satisfaction in knowing you helped position the organisation for long-term success. No one wants to leave and then watch their former organisation crumble and fold due to poor planning or management. The only way to try and assure that does not happen is to be very involved in the hand-off prior to your leaving.

## When succession planning is a surprise

Of course, succession planning assumes that leaving the company is your decision, and that is not always the case today. When companies downsize and employees are made redundant, you can still get a feeling of satisfaction by handing off your responsibilities to the person who will be picking up your position. Training your successor is a form of succession planning and, while done at a faster pace than long-term leadership planning, helping others understand your role, your responsibilities, and the systems you created to ensure the key performance outcomes are met, helps the organisation to continue to be successful.

Granted, training someone else to undertake your role when you had no immediate plans of leaving can be painful and awkward. It is for everyone; however, those individuals who can put aside their hurt and pitch in to help those who will assume their responsibilities frequently earn the well-deserved gratitude of their former colleagues. Not only can this lead to a positive recommendation from the human resources department or your former boss, but having a reputation as a strategic person who puts the needs of the company first can only help you land the position you were meant to have. Your maturity and helpfulness cannot go unnoticed – it will be so unusual – and word will spread to other companies looking for someone just like you.

Keep in mind that leaving one position – whether planned or unplanned – is your opportunity to do what you have always wanted to do. Despite being unexpected, career transition usually leads to employment or a work situation that is a better fit for you.

# Chapter 8
# Emotional Support

*"Life isn't about waiting out the storm;*
*it's about learning to dance in the rain."*
– Anonymous

Transitions require change, and change is stressful, even when that change is moving you in a positive direction. Experiencing change – transition - is likely to cause some degree of depression and anxiety. That is the nature of change and of the sense of a loss of control. We all want to feel in control of our lives, and transitioning from one life situation to another is a time when we are certainly not in control of what comes next. For many executives, that can lead to feeling confused, alone, and scared.

While these emotions are completely natural, negativity has a tendency to get in the way of progress. Some executives report feeling stuck or defeated as they work through where they should be headed. Without support – emotional support – those feelings can worsen and disrupt any kind of career transition. For that reason, it is important to turn to others for comfort, encouragement, guidance, and reassurance.

Those others can be family, friends, colleagues, neighbours, as well as coaches, therapists, counsellors, and spiritual advisors, to name a few. Your supporters should be people who know you and who you trust and respect. You do not need people who will simply pat you on the back and tell you all will be well. You need people who will remind you of your strengths, help you brainstorm career options you might not have considered, offer honest feedback that helps you work through your fears, and envision the life you are working to create.

## Self-Awareness comes first

While surrounding yourself with a support system is critical during transition, successful transition truly starts with you.

To be self-aware is to have the capacity to recognise how your feelings and emotions impact on your personal opinions, attitudes, and judgements. As an emotionally intelligent leader, you will be aware of your emotional experience and know what you are feeling most of the time. It is about having the capacity to recognise how your feelings and emotions impact on your personal opinions, attitudes, and judgements.

*"Knowing others is intelligence; knowing yourself is true wisdom.*
*Mastering others is strength; mastering yourself is true power."*
- Tao Te Ching

Your own emotional intelligence – the ability to recognise, evaluate, and control your emotions – can play a major role in how you process and accept the changes around you. Four key emotional intelligence factors that aid successful career transition are:

- empathy
- relationship skills
- confidence
- optimism

Together they help you create and nurture a support network and approach the process of transition with hope and excitement.

*Empathy*

Empathy is "tuning in" (being sensitive) to what, how, and why people feel and think the way they do. Being empathetic means, being able to "emotionally read" other people. As an empathetic person, you care about others and show interest in and concern for them.

Empathy is the ability to be non-judgmental and put into words your understanding of the other person's perspective on the world, even if you do not agree with it, or even if you find that perspective ridiculous.

At its core, empathy is the ability to see the world from another person's perspective, the capacity to tune in to what someone else might be thinking and feeling about a situation – regardless of how that view might differ from your own perception. Empathy is an extremely powerful interpersonal tool.

Your ability to empathise, to relate to how others are feeling, can help you establish new relationships. Your support system can grow and expand as you come in contact with others and forge personal connections. Those bonds can be formed only if you can recognise what others may be thinking and feeling.

*Relationship skills*

Empathy is one skill essential to forming relationships, but trust, communication, respect, and conflict resolution are essential for maintaining relationships. Building relationship consciousness requires understanding and identifying the key relationships in your business, and using practical strategies for leveraging them to improve the business. Good relationships with a wide range of people are necessary in your career transition; and specific skills are involved to improve social effectiveness. The first skill is awareness of the social environment and the second is good listening skills.

Turning to others for emotional support requires that you be able to feel comfortable sharing what you are going through. The encouragement or commiseration with others needs to come from people you respect and trust, or else you will discount what they have to say.

*"No single factor predicts the productivity of an employee more clearly than his or her relationship with a direct supervisor."*
- Gallup Organisation

Martyn Newman, author of Emotional Capitalist says, to be effective, your relationship skills need to fulfil three conditions:

*Equality*

Relationships work best when you recognise and treat people as equals.

*Mutuality*

People collaborate with you and work well with you, when you provide wins or benefits for them. The more confident you are in your skills and abilities the easier it will be for you to collaborate with other.

*Empowerment*

People work best when they own the relationship by having the freedom to contribute to it.

*Optimism*

Despite the fact that change can be uncomfortable and sometimes unwelcome, if your attitude is positive and you approach the process confident that you will emerge successful, your odds of being successful are nearly 100%. People want to help people who are optimistic and positive, so your emotional support system will function more effectively if you maintain a positive outlook on life and on your transition.

> *"The optimist proclaims that we live in the best of all possible worlds, and the pessimist fears this is true."*
> James Branch Cabell, 1926

Optimism is your ability to look at the brighter side of life and maintain a positive attitude, even in the face of adversity. Optimistic persons can see the big picture and have a vision of where they are going. They are characterised by three attitudes: they look for the benefit in every situation, especially when they experience setbacks; they seek the valuable lesson in every problem or difficulty; and they focus on the task to be accomplished rather than on negative emotions such as disappointment or fear.

As you progress through your career transition it is important to strengthen your resilience so that nothing can disturb your peace of mind. Think only of the best, work only for the best, and expect only the best. Live in the faith that the whole world is on your side, as long as you stay true to the best that is in you.

## Coping with negative emotions

Being optimistic can be a challenge, however. Changing employment, even when it is your choice and may involve a significant promotion or positive step forward, can be unnerving. Transitions of all kinds

71

can be the catalyst for emotional upheaval that may surprise you. Expected and unexpected, good and bad, change elicits an emotional response. Understanding that change can be both exciting *and* scary, an affirmation of your talent *and* nerve-wracking, can help you recognise emotions that may surface and prepare to deal with them effectively. When change is occurring following a corporate-wide restructuring, feelings of sadness and grief are understandable – you are forced to react to it rather than deciding for yourself that you wanted change. But even when you actively choose to pursue a different career path, it is an emotional time. Fear is present when change is initiated or when it is thrust upon you; and that is okay.

Here are some approaches to dealing with your fear:

- Find a career counsellor. Firstly, turn to a professional career counsellor or life coach if you are unsure what your next step should be. The unknown is especially terror-inducing, and finding someone to guide you through the many options you have, or that you should be considering, will help reduce your stress level and help you think more clearly. Your employer's human resources department may be able to recommend someone, or do some research on your own online to find someone to work with you on your career plan. While you may feel out of sorts right now, a professional can point you in the right direction and help you overcome fear and grief.
- Get to work. Secondly, while you may not have a job to report to at the moment, there are plenty of steps you can and should be taking to prepare for your next assignment. Update your curriculum vitae, work on your cover letter, be in touch with recruiters and head hunters, explore careers online, sign up for job search services, start networking with professional groups, call colleagues about openings they may be aware of
- Get busy. Not only will activity improve your mood, but it will move you closer to finding what you were meant to be doing.

- Look for a support group. If you have recently been made redundant or sacked, you may be reeling from the unexpected event. That is understandable. But you are not alone and, in fact, there may be many people in your exact same situation. Look for organised groups of former employees or of people in transition. They do exist and it can be comforting to be amongst people who have experienced what you have. They can also provide advice, suggest resources, and share job opportunities within the group. Check with your organisation's human resources department and conduct an online search to see what you turn up. Some companies have "alumni" groups consisting of former employees, which is another type of group to seek out.
- Surround yourself with people who care about you. The best way to bounce back from negative emotions and doubts is to spend time with people you like and trust. Be honest with them about how you are doing and how you are feeling. Sometimes simply stating what you are feeling can be quite a relief. Rely on your support system – your inner circle – to help you recover from any feelings of fear or overwhelm by spending time with them. They will be there to cheer you on, to encourage you, to offer honest advice, and to pick you up when you have had a bad day. This group of friends and family is essential, so let them know straight away what you are coping with so that they can step in and help. Unless you tell them what you are going through, they cannot provide the support you need.
- Focus on what you know. Since anxiety and fear often stem from the unknown, remind yourself of what you do know about where you are and where you are going. Make a mental list of what is going right in your life – you have a home, friends and family who care about you, a bank account that is in credit, skills others have recognised, an industry reputation, a track record of success. Then run through what you expect

to come up in the near future. You may have interviews – some will go well some will not. You may be offered a position in another city. You may decide you would like to retire right now. Or perhaps start a business. Consider what the worst-case scenario is, and you will undoubtedly realise your worst-case is not so bad after all.

- Act positive. Research has shown that wallowing in fear or negativity is not productive. It does not help you get it out of your system or recover from feeling gloomy and depressed. If you insist on remaining sad and down, you will stay there. Conversely, if you take steps to elevate your mood, you will actually feel better. It's the old "fake it 'til you make it" adage. If you want to feel more hopeful and optimistic, start talking like someone who is hopeful and optimistic. When you dwell on your challenges, you will experience more challenge, so stay focused on what you want instead of challenges. Your thoughts create your reality. Get up and get dressed for networking or meetings. Schedule lunch dates with friends and colleagues. Take steps – literally – to improve your outlook.

Taking steps to regain control of your life and your emotions will help you keep moving through your transition, toward the career that will bring you joy and fulfilment.

## Communicating your needs

The key to receiving the kind of emotional support you want and need from your inner circle is to communicate what you want and ask for ideas on how they can help. Some days you may want someone to bounce ideas off or to provide an alternate perspective on a situation, and other days you may simply want to be left alone. Only you know how you are feeling and what you want – others are unable to anticipate your needs – so make sure you let friends and family know the resources and support that you need.

Letting them know you would like to have some time to yourself is perfectly acceptable. Problems, however, will arise if you indicate you are happy to get together and then spend the whole evening in the corner sulking because you don't really want to be there. In such situations, that is not fair to your friends. Be honest about your limits, about what you are comfortable doing and what you are not comfortable doing on any particular day. Your friends will understand, as long as you tell them.

## Dealing with others' reactions

While you may thrilled to be exploring new career opportunities and have a plan in place to move you in that direction, those around you may be more resistant to change. Your immediate family may be less excited about your career change than you are, so be aware of that. While you may perceive the opportunity to change fields, change companies, or even change the focus of your work life from corporate to non-profit to be rewarding and thrilling, your partner or spouse may need some time to adjust to the change. In some instances, immediate family members may be the ones focused on what they have lost – stability, routine, solid finances – and need time to adapt to the fact that change is coming.

One way to reduce such fear and discomfort is to spread your transition period over a longer period of time, rather than trying to get it over with as soon as possible. Talk frequently with your partner and children (that is if children are part of your family structure) about what you are doing, where you are heading, and what to expect next. If you are going on an interview with a firm, let them know that you are pursuing new employment – but it may be best to hold back on many of the specifics. If you have received an offer for employment, discuss it with your partner and ask for plenty of time to make a decision, so you can prepare your family. Ask for sufficient time, even when scheduling a start date, to allow for everyone to adjust.

## Keeping yourself accountable

At some point in their work lives, many executives begin to ponder what else they could be doing. They wonder what else is out there that they might enjoy more than their current position, or that they would be better at. This questioning and self-evaluation is often the catalyst for career transition.

For some executives, the realisation that they are not in the optimal position or career can be like a lightning bolt, prompting feverish action to initiate change. They want change now, immediately, despite the upheaval and havoc it may wreak. This sudden, unplanned career transition does not always end well because it is not well thought out. Planning, assessing, making steady progress ahead is generally the most successful approach to transition.

On the other hand, there is such a thing as inactivity. That early momentum, and excitement of picturing what could be, can sometimes give way to complacency and acceptance of the status quo. Many executives who know they would be happier elsewhere fail to take steps to initiate change because they know it will be difficult. They get scared and they back off their inquiries and evaluations and decide to stay put. That approach is not rewarding, because they could be so much more satisfied elsewhere, if they just took the time to imagine a different work life. That is where their support team – their family, friends, and close associates – have a part to play.

If you are serious about transitioning out of your current situation, enlist the help of your supporters to be accountable. Think of them as your accountability team, who will support you as you transition. They are there to check in with you, to encourage you, to offer ideas and to prod you when you seem to get stuck or are questioning your decision. They won't let you fall back or give up or wallow.

Too many executives give up too quickly, wanting major change to arrive in a matter of days or weeks. Transition does not happen that way. It is a process that takes mental and emotional work and stamina. If you find yourself feeling weary of the work, check in with your support group to get back on track. There is no reason to be unfulfilled, bored, or unemployed. It will just take a bit more effort to get where you are going.

# Chapter 9
# Networks and Networking

*"You can make more friends in two months by becoming interested in other people than you can in two years by trying to get other people interested in you."*
- Dale Carnegie

Career transition is much easier, faster, and more productive with the help of a network of colleagues, acquaintances, former bosses, university chums, influencers, neighbours, mentors, and friends. With the help of people who know, like, and trust you, you can quickly be referred to others who may be offering employment or who may know someone else who is. Your network is your gateway to the career you were meant to have.

It has been said that most professionals have a network of at least 250 people so, if you tap into your own network, in theory, you are gaining access to more than 62,500 people. Building relationships with those with whom you have connections is a much more effective strategy for finding your next position than sending CVs to apply for employment openings. According to a recent LinkedIn report titled, "Hire Economics: Why Applying to Jobs Is a Waste of Time", Lou Adler says, *'the vast majority of jobs are either filled internally through promotions or lateral moves, or through referrals and recommendations from those within the organisation. Consequently, those in transition are strongly advised to spend no more than 20 percent of their time applying for posted jobs and the remaining 80 percent networking. Odds are high that your next job will result from a connection you already have rather than an advertisement you spot in the newspaper or online.'*

## The Rules of Networking

An essential way of bringing about change through your career transition is to extend your own network of influence and credibility through building more effective relationships with people. Networking is all about making new connections and strengthening old relationships through communication. The most effective networkers are constantly reaching out to broaden their circle of contacts and to remain memorable within others' networks. But there is a right way and a wrong way to network – or perhaps an effective and ineffective way. The first thing you have to do, therefore, is to listen to others well and to ask them interesting questions. Listening can be a key way of influencing people because:

a) Listening empowers – it helps explore and clarify your thinking, identify what is getting in your way; listening helps you to deal with your feelings and then move forward.
b) Listening helps you discover that, behind all the feelings of fear, hopelessness, or powerlessness, at the other side there is a vision of how your ideal career transition might be. Listening helps you discover your vision, and puts you in touch with your potential to be visionary.
c) Through expressing some of your feelings, listening to others helps you deal with your feelings and start to move forward.
d) It is the best – and most exciting – way to get your significant others feeling involved.
e) It is the best way to enable you to see your whole situation, build an accurate perception of reality, *and* to end your own isolation.

Once you start listening to others in this way, trust will develop, and it may be appropriate for you to share your vision with them too.

**Analysing Your Network –I use the following exercise in my executive coaching sessions:**

1. Make a list of the people who work around you – your bosses, your team, and your peers – people who are above, around and below you. Make it a long list.
2. Label each of them as "F", "E" or "C" according to the kind of contact you have with them:
   **Formal:** Either you have to deal with them or they are in a formal position to help you.
   **Experts:** They have information or experience you need.
   **Carriers:** They are in a position to carry the message, bring about change, and
   **Influencers:** influence others.
3. Who, on your list, do you really trust? Who trusts you? Mark them with a "T."
4. Review the names on your list and now think about the action you need to take with each person with whom it is important to build your relationship and bring into the "trust" category. Note the steps you need to take in the action column.

**Developing Your Network**

Now think about the people on your list as one of three categories and plot them into the appropriate circle:

**Inner Circle:** The key people with whom you aim to develop the closest possible collaborative relationships. You will regularly listen to them and teach them to listen to you. Probably 6-12 people who will be your closest allies.

**Middle Circle:** Those who you will aim to build as allies but with whom you will not reckon to spend large amounts of time. Not major sources of support for you but perhaps key people or important clients.

**Outer Circle:** Those who you will have a long-term goal of bringing in or who you need to keep in touch with – possibly in non-time consuming ways.

**This process overall will ensure that:**
(1) You invest your time in building the most important and productive relationships – working smart not hard.
(2) You get support for yourself.
(3) You utilise other people to influence and bring about change, rather than trying to do it all on your own.

Here are some ideas for you to act on and some to avoid as you mix and circulate:

*Do*

**Prepare an elevator speech.** An elevator speech is that 10-15-second description of who you are and what you do, which can be delivered in full between floors on a lift. It is succinct, highlights what you have to offer an organisation, and ends with a question about the other person. That inquiry might be about what the other person does, what their role is at the company, or a broader question, such as what they like to do for fun.

**Show true interest in other people.** When meeting others for the first time, pay attention to what they tell you about themselves. Focus on remembering what you have heard rather than preparing for what you are going to say next. Listening and gathering information about others will serve you well by helping you demonstrate that you were paying attention when they were speaking (which too few people do).

82

**Use a contact management system.** Keep track of who you know and who you have met with a contact management system or simple spreadsheet that allows you to enter new information about them as you learn it. There is a system that scans business cards and records the information on them, or there is a software program like ACT that permits you to enter information manually. Name, email, phone, and employer should be collected at a minimum, but you may also want to note where you met each individual, what their partner's name is, what their children's names are, what you talked about, and more. These details help you build on that first interaction.

**Schedule informational interviews.** Many executives are willing to dialog with others who may be considering employment within their firm. Such discussions can be helpful in determining if the culture is a good fit with your personality and lifestyle. The purpose is simply to share information to aid in your transition and potential employment search – there is no commitment to help find you employment or serve as a reference. In terms of getting an insider's perspective on how the organisation functions, however, this is an excellent tool.

**Share what you know.** After establishing contact, do not wait for the other person to offer assistance – or even to recognise how they can help you. Instead, be on the lookout for information that may be of interest or use to them. Email interesting blog posts, articles, or news briefs related to the industry, employment position, or outside interest of any of your new acquaintances. This not only reminds them of your existence but also sparks a feeling of gratitude that you thought of them. Then, when you turn to them for guidance, your odds of receiving help are much higher.

**Say thank you.** If someone is willing to share their expertise or make introductions for you, the very least you can do is express appreciation in a handwritten note. Not only does this position you as someone with class, but it makes the recipient more likely to want to continue to assist you. No one likes an ingrate.

*Avoid*

**Making the conversation all about you.** Networking is a two-way street. You share information, you receive information. Ideally, by asking questions and being interested in what others have to say, you gather more information from your new acquaintance than they gather from you. If you find that you are talking more than your new contact, stop. Start asking questions instead, for example, what is working well for you? What is difficult? How do you want to change things? Keeping the focus on yourself is likely to make the other person want to walk away from you.

**Waiting for others to reach out to you.** After expressing your interest in changing careers, joining a new firm, or finding new employment, you may think your networking is done. It is not. You need to be continually following up to remind others of your employment search. You need to take the initiative to check in, to offer interesting information, and to thank them for anything they have done already to assist you.

**Leading with the fact that you are in transition.** Introducing yourself as someone who is in transition may put others off. Starting a conversation with the fact that you are currently looking for employment that makes better use of your skill-set presents you as someone in need of something, which is a position of weakness. Despite the fact that you may be more experienced and have a more impressive resumé than people you are interacting with, if you start the conversation with, "I'm in transition and looking for a new position in the X industry," you may see people scatter. That is most likely because others who have come before you have been overbearing and annoying in how they behaved, so don't be lumped in the same category with them. Make sure to mention what you are good at, what you have accomplished, and what you have been doing in your last employment position.

**Limiting your networking to existing organisations.** If you are considering a career transition or are already exploring new opportunities, make sure you are taking the opportunity to travel in circles you don't normally. For example, attend meetings of industry associations you may not typically frequent. Find gatherings of like-minded people to connect with. Look for groups that may have connections with organisations you may want to work with, and then dive in to get in front of group members. Getting together with the same friends and work associates may be fun and comforting, but it does not help expand your network.

## Talking Points

Starting a conversation can feel awkward, especially when in the company of strangers. But when those strangers may be your path to your next position, you will need to put aside your discomfort and find a way to network with them. The most helpful step is to go in prepared with questions – questions you can pose of others to learn more about them and to gather information that may be useful in your employment search. Some of the best questions to pose have to do with:

- Your personal interests and those of the people around you
- News as it relates to the company you are exploring or the industry you may want to move into
- What your acquaintance does and loves about their job and/or company
- Volunteer work they do
- Conferences or professional development seminars they have recently attended
- What they would choose to do if money were no object

Although you certainly do not want your acquaintance to feel as if you are cross-examining them, or peppering them with questions, if you can alternate between sharing your perspective on topics and asking for feedback or the thoughts of others, you will benefit from hearing what they have to say on a wide variety of topics.

## Expanding Your Network

So how can you tap into that larger group of people who may be willing to recommend you for an opening within their company? Be where they are. Of course, firstly, you need to find out where they congregate and, secondly, you need to go where they are. If you discover a particular pub or wine bar is where employees at one company always head after work on Fridays, make sure you are there. If you learn that certain recruitment managers are active in a local professional association, sign up to attend the next meeting. If you know that leaders in your industry support a particular charitable organisation, consider volunteering alongside them.

Just as salespeople go where their prospects are likely to be, you need to go where your future employer is likely to be. Research meetings, events, parties, and other affairs where they may turn up – and then go there. I am not advocating stalking anyone, only researching where your best job prospects or influencers are and then travelling in those circles.

## Expanding your affiliations

In order to meet new people to add to your professional network, it helps to become active in a variety of networking groups. These include but are not limited to:
- Industry-specific organisations, such as for finance or manufacturing
- Groups for professional fields, such as marketing or accounting

- Alumni chapters, such as for universities or corporate employers
- Charitable organisations, such as Oxfam or Save the Children
- Organisations for women only, such as the International Federation of Business and Professional Women or Junior League
- Local groups, such as for young professionals or CEOs
- Sports clubs, such as for cricket or rowing
- Groups for professionals in transition

The more different groups you participate in, the greater the variety of people you will come in contact with, and the larger and more diverse your network will grow.

This helps avoid the challenge of starting to network only after you have been made redundant, or once you have decided you can no longer stand to remain on staff at your current employer. It is always more difficult to begin meeting new people when you are in transition. **Note the following, wherever you are in your search for employment, for a more fulfilling career, start networking now.**

### Asking for references

At some point during the process of searching for your new employment, someone will ask for professional references. That is, they want to hear what others have to say about you including your skills, your managerial style, and your past accomplishments. If you are still gainfully employed it may be unwise for you to ask your current boss for a reference to a potential new employer; that would be awkward and might put your current employment in jeopardy. So you will need to turn to others who know you well in a professional capacity – your network.

As you prepare a list of potential references, think about people you have worked with, volunteered with, worked for, and who have worked for you. These people should all be part of your network and feel very comfortable discussing your strengths and downplaying any weaknesses. If you are not sure what someone would say about you, they are not a good choice to serve for your testimonial. Opt instead for someone who knows you better.

Successful career transition starts with you and your exploration of what type of professional role would be most satisfying, and then moves into information gathering and sharing with others as you evaluate your many options. That is where your network can be most useful, both in providing information and pointing you to others who can give you what you need information-wise. If you are not getting what you need, it is time to expand your network to include a wider range of contacts and colleagues.

# Chapter 10
# Giving Back

*"You have everything you need for complete peace
and total happiness right now."*
-Wayne Dyer

**"The average adult spends much of his or her life working, as much as a quarter or perhaps a third of his waking life in work. As much as a fifth to a quarter of the variation in adult life satisfaction can be accounted for by satisfaction with work". Campbell, Converse & Rodgers, 1976**

Sensible career management is essential in order to enhance your satisfaction in work, your mental health, and perhaps your overall life satisfaction.

How fulfilling is your current work? If you are in transition because you felt a calling or need to do something new, you are not alone. A U.S. MetLife Foundation/Civic Ventures survey a few years ago reported that half of all workers between the ages of 44 and 70 are interested in pursuing a new career path. Similarly, research at New York University, shows that many workers in their 40s and 50s reach a point in their lives when they desire more meaningful work. Entering the second half of their lives, many executives decide it is time to turn their attention outward, to the world at large. Making a difference is often their mantra – maybe it has become yours as well.

Sadly, too few people are leading their lives – are choosing to make a change and make a difference. Most are letting their lives lead them, accepting whatever happens as destiny. As a result, they have lives that are unfulfilling and unsatisfying, unaware that the life they dream of is within their grasp. All it takes is the willingness to transition from life as it is to life as you want it to be. That is where you are now.

## Finding your passion

To start on your path of having a fulfilling career and life, you need to figure out what it is that you are passionate about. It may be your work, or it may be your church or synagogue or mosque, it may be the volunteering you do weekly at your local animal shelter or the painting class you take on Saturdays. What is it that you could do all day long and love every minute? That is what you need to be doing if you do not currently feel that way about your main employment. You need to find a way to spend more time doing what you are passionate about and less time at what is currently filling your days.

Often the best place to start is with your gut, your intuition. What is your gut telling you about where you will be happiest? Is it at home taking care of your children or grandchildren? Is it helping out at schools serving underprivileged children? Is it teaching classes in prisons? Is it building homes in Africa? Or is it moving into a new area within your current company, perhaps even taking a demotion or lateral move to gain balance in your life? Transitioning does not require that you wipe the slate clean and do something totally different from what you are doing now. Maybe what you need is only slightly different from what you currently have. You are the only one who can figure that out. So what is it that your gut, or that little voice in your head, is suggesting you should explore?

The ideas that come to you, or that your gut suggests would be a good fit, may make no sense at first. Note your ideas rather than ignore them, even if they seem crazy. Your instinct is your subconscious mind trying to make you aware of what your heart truly desires. What comes to you may seem silly or impossible, but it is likely close to what would make you happiest. Consider what it would take to make that vision a reality.

## Avoiding employment hopping

One strategy that will not move you forward or allow you to find what you were meant to do is moving too quickly. Career transition takes time. Allowing yourself the time and space to truly consider your own happiness does not happen overnight. For that reason, jumping too soon to accept new employment, move to a new town, or make some other major change is unlikely to result in long-term happiness. You may think you have found love-at-first-sight but it is more likely that you have found a distraction from what's not working at the moment. Do avoid distraction.

Making a decision to accept the first new employment that is offered to you likely reflects how unhappy you are in your current position. Just because you are making a change does not mean that it is a good change, or a positive change. It is merely a change to get away from what you have that you do not like. Stay true to your mission of finding whatever it is that will truly fill you up and give you pleasure.

While you may be more focused on evaluating the salary, benefits, location, amount of travel, and other features of employment you are considering, take a step back. These may impact how comfortable your life is, but they have nothing to do with your sense of fulfilment and satisfaction. As the saying goes, "Money isn't everything." Truthfully, it may not be the number one priority. That is not to say you need to take a vow of poverty, or to significantly undersell your skills and abilities but only that the money should not be your first consideration when evaluating different career opportunities.

What *does* matter is how you feel about the work you would be doing. If you are serious about a healthy lifestyle, working for a company that manufactures and markets cigarettes or cigars is not likely to bring you satisfaction. If you are a recovering alcoholic, a beer distributor or liquor marketer would not be the best choice, for several reasons. Or if the environment is high on your list of things we should protect, a logging operation or oil company might not match up well with your priorities. To be sure that you feel good about what you do on a daily basis and over the course of your career, be clear about what matters to you and make sure it also matters to your next employer, whoever that is. If there is a lack of synchronicity between what matters to you and the employment position, your next career move may be short-lived or not as fulfilling as you had hoped and planned.

## Leaving a legacy

For some executives in transition, leaving a legacy is foremost in their minds. Not just securing an employment position, or their next, but finding the employment position that can make a difference long-term. Your legacy is how you will be remembered. What will you be known for generations from now? What can you leave behind? Will your legacy still be making a positive impact on your community?

Concerned that their lives may not be making the difference they desire, some executives transition into what are frequently called "encore careers", or new career directions that may be completely different from what they had been doing. Some retire and become active with not-for- profit organisations, others go back to university for training in an entirely new livelihood, and some continue in a leadership role but do so in a new industry. I recently met a former senior investment banker who completely retrained and is now working as an osteopath. He is highly engaged and passionate about muscular-skeletal health, and he clearly is giving something back to society. Other persons may volunteer their time, skills, and expertise. Volunteering makes a massive difference to communities and individual persons. The options are unlimited, but deciding to move in a new career direction is fairly common today as executives search for ways to ensure their lives have meaning. Giving back to their community, to enrich those around them, becomes a theme.

**Ways to give back**

Although "giving back" has financial connotations, the phrase actually has a broader meaning. There are a number of ways you can contribute to the good of your local community or to humanity. Here are some of the most popular:

- **Charitable deeds.** Joining the board of directors of a worthy not-for-profit organisation you support can be fulfilling. Taking on a leadership role within an agency or charity you respect can provide a sense of meaning and an appreciation for what you have – the life you have built for yourself. Becoming involved in the oversight of the organisation can provide a way to assist the not-for-profit organisation while allowing you to apply the knowledge and experience you have gained in your career. If you are unsure which of several not-for-profit organisations you may wish to support, join a committee or volunteer for an upcoming event to see if there is a fit with your personality and work style. Test the waters before committing to a multi-year role on a board or in a leadership capacity.
- **Service projects.** Participating in local service projects within the community – short-term or one-day events – is another way that you can play an active role in improving the quality

of life of your region without making a longer-term commitment. This could be anything from clean-up of a polluted area to assisting in a blood drive to making a presentation at a TED session. Consider what types of projects interest you and how you can best apply your knowledge as you explore the opportunities available.

- **Mentor.** Serving as a mentor to someone in need of direction or coaching can be a very rewarding way to give back, by aiding young people in improving their lives. You can mentor junior employees in your company, troubled youth, children without parents, university students beginning to think about future careers, or anyone who is in need of guidance. Many local organisations are looking for experienced, successful mentors like you to offer encouragement and life lessons.

- **Government participation.** Putting yourself forward for a government position or appointment is another way to share your talents and interests with the larger community. Most politicians start at the local level, such as borough/town or city council, and work their way up, but you may decide to jump right in and run for Mayor. Where you start is up to you and your sense of the amount of support you would need to be successful. By tapping into your network, you should be able to get a fairly accurate sense of your chances straight away.

- **Establishing a new organisation.** Starting a new organisation to address a concern or need is another approach. Should you be unsuccessful in locating a not-for-profit organisation or other group dedicated to serving a particular group of people, or working to eradicate a certain illness or improve a particular aspect of life, you may consider creating your own foundation or not-for- profit organisation. Your goal could be to galvanize splintered organisations to pool your resources and make a bigger difference. Or maybe you see a gaping hole in serving a particular group and want to fix that. If you cannot find a group that fits your particular interests and passion, by all means, start your own.

- **Going abroad.** If you have been struck by the conditions elsewhere, outside of your country, your work may involve travelling to countries in need of support. Whether through religious organisations with scheduled mission trips, or through travel groups dedicated to making a difference, there are plenty of opportunities to improve the lives of others of the world with less economic prosperity. The dollar, pound and the euro are often stronger currencies than the currencies of countries with less economic prosperity, so to that end your finances can have a much larger impact in third-world locations.

- **Investing.** Financially supporting an organisation or a particular initiative is perhaps the most common way executives choose to give back, especially when they are still working within a corporation. Without free time, they give what they can – money. Furthermore, that money can make radical change possible for others. So perhaps you can give back by continuing to work in employment that you love but investing a portion of your income to do good deeds elsewhere too. Nearly every not-for-profit organisation could make good use of any amount of money you would choose to donate. Some donors even elect to start their own campaign or to earmark funds for a particular purpose, such as a scholarship fund or a building, for example. Money is a powerful way to make a difference and to give back.

Although many executives use their financial resources to start making a difference, giving money is not as important or effective as giving their time, attention, and/or reputation. Putting their support behind a particular charity or movement can open doors previously closed, by catching the attention of prominent individuals who may also like to help. Just as celebrities preferring particular brands of clothing or furniture or water can mean increased sales of those brands, executives demonstrating preference for particular causes and organisations can have a similar effect. Executives can leverage their own reputation and resources to encourage and entice others to support agencies, organisations, events, fundraisers – whatever the cause.

## Your life is like a book

Every connection you make, every employment position you have held or work you have done in support of a particular organisation is your legacy. Each stage of your life is a chapter, each milestone its own section. Your life is a record of your noble purpose, of what you tried to achieve to better mankind. **How do you want your life story to end?** It's your choice.

What you do next is completely your choice. Whether you rush toward something new, whether you take the time you need to ponder your next move, whether you turn to your support system for guidance, whether you throw yourself into a cause or group that is important to you – you have a choice. That choice will lead you to your next chapter, whatever it is. Your career transition is your chance to change the plot of your story, to chart the summit that you will climb and the altitude at which you will fly, to change its ending. Capitalise your legacy. Choose the flight path that will make you happiest and you will be given the opportunity to make others happy.

# Free Bonus

**Do you want more!**
- More success in your career?
- More happiness?
- More energy?
- More productivity
- More vibrant health
- Clarity and consistency in your life?
- Living life on your terms?
- Looking towards each day with joy and fulfilment?

Neslyn Watson-Druée, 1 of 200 elite *Certified High Performance Coach*™ in the world offers you a free high performance coaching strategy session. If you have just 20 minutes to fill in a questionnaire, then Neslyn will teach you:

- How the world's most accomplished and influential people **THINK**
- Why you have been so exhausted (and what you can do about it immediately)
- Why most people **FAIL** at managing their time and day
- The number 1 secret you most follow to have more influence with people
- How to define your purpose, get rid of distraction, and finally gain momentum in life.

Neslyn knows that it is your deep desire to have more success and keep everything together. So, Neslyn will teach you **six** simple principles that you can use to better master your mind, body and ability to become more productive and persuasive.

These strategies that will **completely** change how you feel,
manage your day, and influence others.

Neslyn wants to give you the exact strategies and questions the world's most accomplished and influential use to manage their emotions, schedule their days, persuade others, and keep their passions and purpose clear and alive. Knowing these will transform your life.

Frankly, if you are not following the six principles, then it is almost impossible to get ahead these days. If it is your time for a dramatic change and rapid advancement in your personal and professional life, then Neslyn would like to work one-on-one with you to break through your barriers and help you reach your highest potential and performance in all you do.

To begin, and to see if you qualify, just follow the instructions right now:

1. **Send an email** to ceocareertransition@gmail.com **requesting free strategy session**
2. On receipt of the questionnaire, Fill out my questionnaire for a free strategy session (NB you can write in the pdf file)
3. **Email your completed questionnaire to:** ceocareertransition@gmail.com
4. **In addition, claim 50% discount on Purpose and Passion Development Day**

Once your answers to your completed questionnaire is reviewed to determine if you are a right fit for high performance coaching, Neslyn will schedule a free one-on-one telephone consultation with you.

**Breakthrough to your full potential Now**

# Supportive Resources to develop your thoughts further:

**Chapter 1** – What Leads To Career Transition:
David Carter, Break Through – *Learn The secrets of the world's leading mentor and become the best you can be.* **Piatkus Books, 2013, ISBN 978-0-7499-5955-5**

**Chapter 2** – Top Five Reasons for Career Transition:
Paul Tillich, *The Courage To Be.* **Yale University Press, 2000, ISBN 978-0-300-08471-9**

**Chapter 3** – Life Balance and the Challenge of Transition:
James Kouzes & Barry Posner, *The Leadership Challenge.* **Jossey-Bass, 1987, ISBN 1-55542-061-3**
*Challenges of Work–Life Balance for Women Physicians/Mothers Working in Leadership Positions.*
**http://www.sciencedirect.com/science/article/pii/S1550857912001040**

**Chapter 4** – Confidence Helps You Manage Transition:
Tim Ursiny, *The Confidence Plan.* **Source Books, INC. Naperville, Illinois, 2005, ISBN 1-4022-0349-7**

**Chapter 5** – Managing Expectations:
Alan Laken, *How To Get Control of Your Time and Your Life*, **Signet,1990, ISBN 0-451-16772-4**

**Chapter 6** – Knowing Yourself:
Larry Stout, *Leadership: From Mystery to Mastery*, **Stockholm School of Economics, 2001, ISBN 9984-590-38-0**
Tom Rath, *Strengths Finder*, **Gallop Press, 2007, ISBN 9781595 620156**

Lumina Leader Profile    }
Lumina Spark Profile     }     contact@beaconorganisationaldevelopment.com
Emotional Capital Report}

**Chapter 7** – Defining Success:
Margaret Wheatley, *Leadership and the New Science: Discovering Order in a Chaotic World*, **Berrette-Koehler, 2006. ISBN978-45877-760-7**
John Maxwell, *The 21 Irrefutable Laws of Leadership*, **Thomas Nelson 2007, ISBN 9-780785 289357**

**Chapter 8** – Emotional Support:
Martyn Newman, *Emotional Capitalists The New Leaders*, **Jossey Bass, 2009. ISBN 978-0-470-69421**

**Chapter 9** – Networking and Networks:
Dorothy Leeds, *Marketing Yourself: How to Sell Yourself and the Get Jobs You've Always Wanted.* **Piatkus 1991. ISBN 9 780749 910532**

**Chapter 10** – Giving Something Back:
Peter Senge et, al., *Presence: Exploring  Profound Change in People, Organisations and Society.* **Nicholas Brealey 2012.**
**ISBN 078-1-65788-355-8**

http://www.bibbycommunity.com/about/item/45-giving-something-back-programme.html

http://freedominternationalNOW.com **Founded by Simon Hedley**

Visit http://ceo-careertransition.com for up-to-date blogs and additional resources

# About The Author

Neslyn Watson-Druée – At the time of publication Neslyn Watson-Druée is one of 200 *Certified High Performance Coach*™ in the world. Neslyn's skills in coaching are grounded in The High Performance Academy™, Thinking Environment™ - Consultant/ Coach, One Command™ Practitioner/ Coach. Neslyn , a *Leadership* Public Speaker – **The Leaders' Code**.

Neslyn has lead her own high performing career transition from Registered General Nurse to Registered Midwife, Public Health Nurse, Higher Education Lecturer, Deputy Director of Nurse Education, Business Owner and Board Member of Various Boards within the British National Health System – inclusive 10 years as Chairman of NHS Kingston. In addition, Neslyn has served on the Board of Tomorrow's People twice in the role of Trustee.

Neslyn is highly decorated with three honours from Her Majesty Queen Elizabeth 11 of the United Kingdom and the Commonwealth as follows:

- Member of the Most Excellent Order of the British Empire
- Commander of the Most Excellent Order of the British Empire
- Queen Elizabeth 11 Medal

A selection of other awards conferred to Neslyn are – Business Excellence Award, Woman In Business Award, Gold Standard Award for Boosting Employee Potential, Training and Consultancy Award, Diversity Persuader of the Decade – British Diversity Awards, Millennium Nurse – Special Recognition Award, Fellowship of the Royal College of Nursing, Windrush Services towards Nursing Innovation Winner, Inaugural Top 50 Pioneers in British NHS from Black and Minority Ethnic Group, Fellowship of The City and Guilds, London Institute, Doctor of the Universities of Birmingham City University and Bradford University.

Neslyn is passionate about enabling and maintaining high performance in career transitions because of the constant climate of change in organisations. There needs to be successful career transitions because:

- 71% of workers are 'not engaged' representing a near-record low. Gallup, 2011
- 84% of senior leaders globally say disengaged employees are one of the three biggest threats facing their business. The Economist
- 'Few things can have as much immediate impact [upon engagement] as an effective relationship with one's direct manager.' (TW) Global Workforce Study, 2012

Neslyn's clients say that working with Neslyn brings about deep transformation because she draws on her wealth of skills and education including those of Business Psychologist, Organisational Development Consultant, One Command™ Leader, PSYCH-K Practitioner and Thought Field Therapist.

The common words Neslyn's clients use to describe her are: inspirational, wise, courageous, creative, spiritual connection, calm, clarity, passionate, commanding - visionary - transformational leader, self-aware, confident, empowering, healing energy, radiation of love, compassion and gratitude. Neslyn's Book on Beacon Leadership will be published early spring 2015.

Made in the USA
Charleston, SC
29 May 2016